Gerald O'Collins, S.J.

Interpreting
the Resurrection

EXAMINING THE MAJOR PROBLEMS
IN THE STORIES OF JESUS' RESURRECTION

PAULIST PRESS
New York/Mahwah, N.J.

Library of Congress Cataloging-in-Publication Data

O'Collins, Gerald.
    Interpreting the Resurrection : examining the major problems in
the stories of Jesus' Resurrection / Gerald O'Collins.
        p.   cm.
    Bibliography: p.
    Includes index.
    ISBN 0-8091-0425-3
    1. Jesus Christ—Resurrection—History of doctrines—20th century.
2. Jesus Christ—Appearances—History of doctrines—20th century.
3. Jesus Christ—Resurrection—Biblical teaching. 4. Jesus Christ—
Appearances—Biblical teaching. 5. Bible. N.T.—Criticism,
interpretation, etc.—History—20th century. I. Title.
BT481.032 1988
232.9'7—dc19   88-25245
                                                          CIP

Published by Paulist Press
997 Macarthur Boulevard
Mahwah, New Jersey 07430

Printed and bound in the
United States of America

Contents

Introduction

The resurrection of Jesus is a profound reality that defies any simple interpretation limited to just one context. It does not present quite the same face in the settings of study, life and prayer. Scholars, sufferers and worshipers rightly appropriate the Easter story in a variety of ways.

Immanuel Kant's *Critique of Pure Reason* may seem of little interest to any but the philosophers. Yet that classic work ends with three questions which retain a permanent validity everywhere. "What can I know? What ought I to do? What may I hope for?"

Those questions readily suggest three major lines of inquiry about the Easter story. What can I know about the historical origins and theological meaning of the resurrection material in the letters of St. Paul, the Gospels and other New Testament books? What ought I to do or leave undone when the story of Jesus' victory over death reads off the movement of my life? What may I hope for when that story becomes my prayer?

The first question invites us to station ourselves in a place of biblical and theological thought—let us say, in the University of Notre Dame, Yale Divinity School or the Gregorian University in Rome. The second question takes us off to the world of action and suffering like the suburbs of Sao Paulo or the streets of New York.

1

The final question could turn us toward the Holy Sepulchre in Jerusalem.

Let us first join the scholars and students in their academic setting. Here we enter a community whose tradition, at least in the Western world, stretches back through the Enlightenment and the achievements of medieval Europe to the glories of ancient Greece. Plato's conversational approach has shaped this tradition for all time. We raise questions, concede points and draw conclusions as the dialogue runs along. Error is the villain and carefully trained reason the solution in the academically rigorous pursuit of truth.

The intellectual approach to Easter scrutinizes the intentions of Paul and the four evangelists, searches out the sources they used and tries to tell at this distance the precise historical events that first gave rise to the proclamation of the crucified Jesus' resurrection. In the best sense of the word "theory," biblical scholars have their theories about the meaning, formation and origins of the Easter texts. They focus on the past in seeking to verify their answers to such questions as: Where did the list of witnesses to the risen Christ come from and how did Paul want to use it (1 Cor 15:5–8)? What were the post-resurrection appearances like? Did the risen Jesus actually eat some fish? Was his tomb found to be open and empty two days after his death and burial? What did Mark mean by the silent flight of the three women at the end of his Gospel (16:8)?

Answers and theories are judged by one's competent use of the available evidence. Truth has the primacy as exegetes practice their academic discipline. Theirs is the work of an intellectual elite. They have enjoyed a privileged education as heirs to the great tradition formed by the old universities of Bologna, Cambridge, Heidelberg, Oxford and Paris.

A second view of the resurrection comes from the *favelas* where people suffer terrible deprivation and struggle to survive. Here it is a matter of consulting the poor, not scholars, about the meaning and message of Easter. In this setting it is not so much intellectual error but injustice, poverty and sin that stand in the way of appropriating the story of Jesus' resurrection.

Stripped to its simplest terms, Easter here means something to be lived and done. The mystery of the crucified Christ rising from the dead calls for a transformation of our world. It invites those who suffer and those who cause their suffering to seek and find a new kind of human existence.

This second way of understanding the resurrection challenges us to "repent and believe in the good news of Jesus' victory over death" rather than to "interpret the Easter narratives more scientifically." We verify the story of the resurrection more by practicing it than by studying it.

The second approach is focused on the here and now—on the present history of suffering, sin and evil. Its vision of Easter takes shape around the question: What good ought I to do for all those for whom Jesus died and rose into final glory?

The holy women at the tomb symbolize a third approach to the resurrection. They come to weep and mourn but find the tomb open and empty. Running back into Jerusalem "with fear and great joy," they meet the risen Jesus and worship him (Mt 28:8–9). They represent all those whose hearts continue to catch fire at the one who died and rose to set us free. On our knees with Mary Magdalene we glimpse the grandeur of God's Son and pray: "Dying you destroyed our death, rising you restored our life. Lord Jesus, come in glory."

Such then are three different but complementary approaches to the Easter story: through the head, the hands and the heart. The scholar studies and analyzes the story for its historical and theological truth. Those who suffer and struggle in the marketplace can let the story enter and enrich their lives like the lower-class Corinthians to whom Paul preached the resurrection of the crucified Jesus (1 Cor 1:26–28; 15:1–11). Finally, the faithful take in the story when they joyfully proclaim, "Lord, by your cross and resurrection you have set us free. You are the Savior of the world."

Easter is the story of the risen Savior who holds out to us the full and final answers in our triple quest for what we can know, what we ought to do and what we may hope for. We can encounter the Savior in the university setting, along the roads of life and in our places of prayer. In him we find the plenitude of truth, the ultimate good and the utterly satisfying beauty of God. It will take all our study, life and worship to know him.

Most of the time this book will station itself in an academic setting as I ask: What were the post-resurrection appearances like? How should we evaluate the role of Mary Magdalene as Easter witness? What should we make of the fish-eating episode in Luke's final chapter (Lk 24:41–43)? What did Mark mean by the silent and fearful flight of the women with which he ended his Gospel? I hope to answer these questions with some degree of competence. Before doing so, however, I want to acknowledge at the outset that in the matter of Christ's resurrection it is not enough to consult the scholars. One must also consult the poor and the worshipers.

Daniel Kendall, S.J. co-authored with me Chapter 2 ("Mary Magdalene as Major Witness to Jesus' Resurrection") which originally appeared in *Theological Studies* 48 (1987) pp. 631–46. Once again I wish to acknowledge and thank this scholar and dear friend. My thanks go also to John Kilgallen, S.J. whose perceptive comments improved Chapters 3 and 4.

With gratitude and affection this work is dedicated to the memory of Joseph Gregory McCarthy. Joe has died but lives to intercede for us as we continue our pilgrimage on the road home to God.

Gerald O'Collins, S.J.
Rome,
May 22, 1988

CHAPTER 1

What Were the Easter Appearances Like?

When they read Paul's list of Easter witnesses in 1 Cor 15:5–8 or study the resurrection narratives in the Gospels, people everywhere naturally ask: What were the appearances of the risen Lord like? What can we say about their form and nature?

This chapter takes up three answers to that question—coming, respectively, from Reginald H. Fuller, Pheme Perkins and Hans Kessler. Fuller's *The Formation of the Resurrection Narratives* (New York, 1971; 2d ed. Philadelphia, 1980) has passed the test of time and established itself as a classic in its field. Perkins' *Resurrection: New Testament Witness and Contemporary Reflection* (London, 1985) and Kessler's *Sucht den Lebenden nicht bei den Toten: Die Auferstehung Jesu Christi* (Düsseldorf, 1985) are important recent works on the resurrection. Their conclusions about the Easter appearances differ in some significant ways. This article will expound and assess those conclusions in search of a workable position about the form and nature of the appearances.

I

Fuller summarizes and defines the resurrection appearances as follows:

5

They were not in their innermost essence incidents open to neutral observation or verification, but revelatory events in which the eschatological and christological significance of Jesus was disclosed, and in which the recipient was called to a particular function in salvation history (p. 48).

The evidence from 1 Corinthians 15, Galatians 1, the Gospels and elsewhere in the New Testament amply supports the five major points in Fuller's statement. The appearances, while (1) not open to neutral observers, were (2) events of revelation which disclosed the (3) eschatological and (4) christological significance of Jesus and (5) called the recipient to a special mission. It is important to note that Fuller does not want to reduce the appearances to a mere communication of meaning *about* Jesus, as if these events disclosed the "eschatological and christological significance" of someone who was simply not present in the events themselves. Fuller has already insisted on the personal involvement and initiative of Jesus himself, calling the appearances "acts in which Christ, or God in Christ, acts in self-disclosure" (p. 32). What Paul experienced on the Damascus Road was "the *self-disclosure* of the Risen One" (p. 47; italics mine).

Fuller stresses the unique quality of the appearances of the risen Jesus: "there are no categories available for the unprecedented disclosure of the eschatological within history" (p. 33). He toys with the possibility of using analogies drawn from mystical experience and, without going into detail, rejects this possibility: "It is . . . impossible to categorize the Easter appearances in any available this-worldly language, even in that of religious mysticism" (*ibid.*). Later we will see how Kessler pauses to examine the value of possible parallels in the experience and language of the mystics.

Threaded through Fuller's reflections on the resurrection appearances is a strong contrast between the this-worldly and historical aspect, on the one hand, and the eschatological and theological aspect, on the other. This conviction makes him reluctant to call these events "objective visions." That language could tamper with their status as belonging to "the eschatological age." Hence Fuller insists that "if we speak of the Easter appearances as visions, it must be clear that we are speaking only of their this-worldly, historical aspect" (*ibid.*).

Of course, it is precisely the "this-worldly, historical" aspect which people have in mind when they ask: What were the Easter appearances like? Fuller himself answers this question, suggesting "very tentatively" that "the form which the self-disclosure of the Risen One took for Paul (and therefore, presumably, also for the recipients of appearances prior to him) was the form of a vision of light" (p. 47). While emphasizing that these appearances are "best defined theologically as 'revelatory encounters,' " Fuller proposes that their "outward, historically definable form is a vision (perhaps a vision of ('light'), accompanied by an audition (i.e., a communication of meaning)" (p. 49).

What of this hypothesis that the Easter appearances "involved visionary experiences of light, combined with a communication of meaning" (p. 48)? Whether or not it took the precise form of an "audition," some "communication of meaning" accompanied the Easter encounters. To put it mildly, Paul and the Gospels make that clear. In any case an encounter in which there was no communication of meaning whatsoever seems unintelligible. Some might distance themselves from the claim that "the form" of the self-disclosure of the risen Christ was the same for Paul and the recipients of appearances prior to him. Here, however, I want to concentrate more on the proposal that the Easter appearances involved experiences of light.

In support of his hypothesis Fuller brings in three pieces of evidence. (1) First of all, in all three narratives of the Damascus road encounter Luke mentions a light from heaven (Acts 9:3; 22:6; 26:13). In the last passage the light which shone round Paul and his traveling companions is said to have been "brighter than the sun." Fuller believes that it is "safe to infer" that the visionary element of light, an item common to all three accounts of Paul's meeting with the risen Jesus, is "pre-Lucan, not redactional" (p. 46). (2) Then Fuller joins various commentators (he mentions W. Kümmel and H. Grass) in referring a Pauline passage to the Damascus road experience: "For it is the God who said, 'Let light shine out of darkness,' who has shone in our hearts to give the light of the knowledge of the glory of God in the face of Christ" (2 Cor 4:6). (3) Finally, like Grass, Fuller finds some supporting evidence in two further references to the "glory" of the risen Lord (1 Cor 15:43; Phil 3:21).

Apropos of (1) it should be observed that even when one establishes that the experience of light on the Damascus road is "pre-Lucan, not redactional," this would still leave the task of showing that the theme went back through the period of the early community telling the story of Paul's conversion (stage two of the tradition) to the very event of his encounter with the risen Jesus (stage one of the tradition). Some scholars agree with Fuller that Acts is historically reliable in reporting Christ's appearance as a vision of shining light. Over this point Joachim Jeremias accepts the reliability of Acts, and like Fuller also believes that such a luminous appearance "may be regarded as typical" of all the previous appearances of the risen Lord.[1] Pheme Perkins does not commit herself over the historical reliability of the luminous element in the Damascus road meeting. In general she agrees that in the three accounts of Paul's conversion Luke "has probably used some earlier sources" (p. 202). In "Paul's Conversion/Call: A Comparative Analysis of the Three Reports in Acts,"[2] C.W. Hedrick argues that in Acts 9:1–19; 22:4–16 and 26:12–18 Luke has respectively adapted, edited and abbreviated a traditional story of Paul's conversion. But he too leaves open the particular question of the vision in shining light. Was that an element in the pre-Lukan source (stage two of the tradition) and even in the historical form of the risen Jesus' self-disclosure to Saul (stage one of the tradition)?

It seems reasonable or at least plausible to hold that the theme of Saul's luminous vision was already found at the pre-Lukan stage. Luke adapts the theme in various ways. In Acts 9:3 and 22:6 the light shines only around Saul; in Acts 26:13 it also flashes around his traveling companions and knocks them down. According to Acts 9:4 and 22:6–7, the bright light from the sky causes Saul to fall to the ground and apparently produces as well his temporary blindness (Acts 9:8–9; 22:11). But in Acts 26:13 even if the "light from heaven" is "more brilliant" than the midday sun, it does not cause blindness. It seems that Luke in his three narratives of Saul's conversion/call is adapting a theme already found in some traditional story of that event: the risen Jesus' self-disclosure in a luminous vision.

Even granted such a conclusion about stage two of the tradition, we have not yet established that the appearance to Saul historically took the form of a vision of light (stage one of the tradition). The problem is that light was "an index of heavenly reality and divine glory in the apocalyptic traditions of the first century" (Perkins, p. 346) and elsewhere. In the source that Luke drew on for his three accounts of Saul's conversion, the language of "light from heaven" could simply have been a *conventional* way of saying that Saul encountered a heavenly reality, the risen Jesus through whom the glory of God was revealed. Rather than necessarily claiming that in actual fact Saul literally experienced a vision of shining light, this language may only have been a way of saying that in meeting the risen Christ, Paul was confronted with the divine glory which no one can see face to face (Ex. 33:17–22).

What of Fuller's other grounds for supposing that the Easter appearance to Saul historically involved an experience of light? Fuller mentions Grass and Kümmel who like him interpret 2 Cor 4:6 as referring to Saul's Damascus road experience. In his Anchor Bible commentary on 2 Corinthians V.P. Furnish names other scholars (J.D.G. Dunn, G.W. MacRae, A. Plummer and H. Windisch) who understand Paul to be speaking of the subjective aspect of his "conversion experience."[3] One can add to the list F.F. Bruce who interprets the talk of light in 2 Cor 4:6 as "a reminiscence of Paul's conversion experience, when 'the glory of that light' from heaven which outshone the sun (Acts 22:11 . . .) blinded his eyes to everything else."[4]

Kessler envisages the possibility of 2 Cor 4:4–6 referring to Paul's encounter with the risen Christ (p. 145), but would not claim that the apostle is speaking of a "conversion experience." In Acts Luke presents the Damascus road encounter as such a conversion experience, but Paul himself interprets the encounter differently (Kessler, p. 157). It was a call and a commission to be the apostle to the Gentiles, something like the "call-visions" of Isaiah or Jeremiah (*ibid.,* p. 154).

Apropos of 2 Cor 4:6 Furnish points out that the account in Acts of Paul's experience introduces "an external blinding light, not an internal and illuminating one" as in 2 Cor 4:6 (p. 250). Furnish continues:

> Moreover, Paul's own most specific comments about his conversion and call (Gal 1:15–16; 1 Cor 15:8) use the language of revelation, not the language of illumination. Therefore, the origin of the imagery of v. 6 is more apt to be Paul's earlier reference to the blindness of *unbelievers* in v. 4 than his personal experience of spiritual illumination at the time of his conversion (p. 251).

In short, the language of light in 2 Cor 4:6 should be referred to in the general Christian experience of conversion, not to Paul's particular experience on the road to Damascus.

This leaves us Fuller's final reason for arguing that the Easter appearances involved experiences of light: two references by Paul to the "glory" of the risen body (1 Cor 15:43; Phil 3:21). In the first case Paul is speaking of the resurrection of the dead in general (1 Cor 15:42) and not attending to the particular case of Christ. Moreover, it is a question of what has been "sown in humiliation" being "raised [not appearing] in glory" (1 Cor 15:43). In the passage Paul has in mind a resurrection "in glory," not an appearance in glory of Christ or of anyone else. In Phil 3:21 Paul expresses the hope that "the body belonging to our humble state" will be given by Christ "a form like that of his own resplendent body." Here at least the apostle does refer directly to the glorious body of the risen Jesus. Nevertheless, the point is the present state of Christ, not of some glorious appearance in light to Paul or anyone else.

In short, while Fuller's general account of the post-Easter appearances is thoroughly acceptable, his particular suggestion about these appearances involving experiences of light remains at least unproven. Let us turn next to Pheme Perkins' account of the risen Lord's appearances.

II

Unlike Fuller but like a number of other scholars,[5] Perkins uses the term "Christophany" when writing of the appearances of the risen Jesus (pp. 83, 86f., 99, 136, 172, 175). Nevertheless, she is reluctant to hazard many conclusions about the way the disciples experienced these appearances.

> We cannot presume to reach the direct experience of those who became convinced that Jesus had been raised, since our earliest sources are reticent in that regard. From Paul we may presume that it is [was?] a spiritual experience that carried with it the conviction of a revelatory encounter with God. Paul sees himself to have been commissioned as much as one of the Old Testament prophets had been (p. 94).

In her own cautious way, Perkins lines up with what Fuller (see above) had said about the appearances as "revelatory events" (= "the conviction of a revelatory encounter with God"), in which "the eschatological and christological significance of Jesus was disclosed" (= Perkins' "Christophanies") and in which "the recipient was called to a particular function in salvation history" (= Paul seeing "himself to have been commissioned as much as one of the Old Testament prophets had been").

In a moment we can examine the way Perkins fills out her reference to "a *spiritual* experience" (italics mine). What of her claim that "our earliest sources" are reticent about "the direct experience of those who became convinced that Jesus had been raised"? Certainly "our earliest sources" do not say much about that experience, but they do consistently speak of an "appearing" (for example, 1 Cor 15:5–8). In general, the New Testament shows a massive preference for the language of sight when reporting or referring to the encounters between the risen Christ and the disciples.[6] This point qualifies the comparison between Paul's commissioning (Gal 1), which took place when he "saw" the risen Christ, and the calling of the Old Testament prophets, which occurred when they received the word of God. Despite Isaiah's vision (Is 6:1–13) and the visionary elements in the call of Ezekiel (1:1–3:27), they were hearers (of the word) rather than seers (of visions). It was exactly the opposite with Paul and the Easter witnesses. The New Testament portrays them much more as having seen the risen Lord rather than as having heard his voice or word.

Perkins downplays the language of sight, claiming that "the early traditions of resurrection" are "auditory and not visionary" (p. 137). To put matters mildly, there is some tension betweeen this claim and several early traditions of resurrection appearances (for example, 1 Cor 9:1; 15:5–8; Lk 24:34). Obviously, however, Perkins does not discount such texts as she admits that "visionary elements are associated with the proclamation of resurrection." Nevertheless, she adds: "But . . . those elements were not of primary significance in establishing the reality of the resurrection and hence were not transmitted as part of the message from the beginning.

What counts is the testimony that the Lord is risen" (*ibid.*) There are claims here that call for qualification. For Peter, Paul and other original witnesses the visionary elements were of primary significance in establishing *for them* the reality of the resurrection (see, for example, Acts 10:40–41; 13:30–31). Moreover, kerygmatic-credal passages like 1 Cor 15:3–5 and Lk 24:34 indicate that visionary elements could be transmitted as part of the message at the beginning. Certainly the auditory testimony that the Lord is risen (for example, Mk 16:6; Rom 10:9) was (and is) supremely important. But that testimony did not feel the need to suppress the visionary elements which were of primary significance in first establishing Jesus' resurrection from the dead.

Later in her book Perkins explains how the appearances of the risen Christ entailed "a spiritual experience." She speaks of "some sort of external vision," yet qualifies such a vision as "an ecstatic experience such as early Christians commonly attributed to the Spirit," an experience "equivalent to other experiences of the Spirit" (p. 198). I doubt both of the central elements in this version of the Easter encounters. In various places (for example, 2 Cor 12:1ff; Acts 10:11; Rev 1:10) the New Testament refers to ecstatic experiences, but never attributes ecstasy to the risen Christ's post-resurrection meetings with his first disciples or with Paul.

Second, like others (for example, Jn 7:39; Acts 8:14–17) Paul writes of common and particular experiences and gifts of the Spirit that were available for Christians in general (for example, Gal 3:2–5; 1 Cor 12:1–13; 14:1–40). When, however, he recalls the appearances of the risen Jesus (1 Cor 9:1; 15:5–8; Gal 1:12,16), he speaks of a special experience restricted to himself and several others that— apart, apparently from the case of the "more than five hundred brethren" (1 Cor 15:6)—gave the recipients the unique, normative role of being apostolic witnesses who testified to their experience of the risen Lord and brought the Church into existence. Other (later) Christians did and do not experience that fundamental meeting with the risen Christ which made Paul, for example, the last to receive the special apostolic mission (1 Cor 15:8). He invites others to live up to the experience of the Spirit which they share in common with him (Gal 3:2–5). But he does not invite them to repeat his fundamental, apostolic experience of the risen Lord. He never remarks to his readers "Christ has appeared" or "Christ will appear to you."

Three texts (Gal 1:16; 2:20; 4:6) are invoked by Perkins to establish her case for holding that the Easter encounters were "equivalent to other experiences of the Spirit" (p. 198). In Gal 1:16 Paul interprets his encounter with the risen Jesus (Gal 1:1) as the fundamental moment of revelation which made him the apostle to the Gentiles: "[God] was pleased [aorist] to reveal his Son to me, in order that I might preach him among the Gentiles." Although the Greek literally says "in me," the context requires the translation "to me" (so the New English Bible, Revised Standard Version). However, as does the New Jerusalem Bible, Perkins maintains "in me" and she links it (a) to Paul's confession "it is no longer I who live but Christ who lives [present] in me" (2:20), and (b) to the apostle's appeal to the Galatian experience of sonship which comes through the indwelling Spirit: "God has sent the Spirit of his Son into our hearts, crying 'Abba! Father!' " (Gal 4:6). The proposal of Perkins is to associate the Son revealed in me (Gal 1:16) and the Christ living in me (Gal 2:20) with the indwelling Spirit (Gal 4:6), so as to interpret the resurrection Christophanies along the lines of common experiences of the Spirit.

This, however, is to confuse what Paul affirms about his being once-and-for-all called to his apostolic special mission (Gal 1:16) with what he indicates about the common Christian experience of the continuing indwelling of the Holy Spirit (Gal 4:6; see also, for example, Rom 5:5; 8:11). Very occasionally, Paul speaks of Christ living "in us," "in you" (Rom 8:10), or "in me" (Gal 2:20). Normally he expresses the new communion of life all Christians enjoy as our being "in Christ" (for example, Rom 8:1; 16:7; 1 Cor 15:22; Phil 3:8–9). Either way, Paul reports the common, ongoing

Christological ("we/I in Christ" or "Christ in us/me") and pneumato-logical ("the Spirit in us/me") experiences of all believers. But these experiences are not the same as the special, once-and-for-all event, "the last and definitive" appearance of the risen Christ which made an apostle of Paul (Fuller, p. 49).

It is interesting to note that in his *Foundations of Christian Faith* (New York, 1978) Karl Rahner also compares the first disciples' experience of the risen Jesus with our experiences of the Holy Spirit: "So far as the nature of this experience is accessible to us, it is to be explained after the manner of our experience of the powerful Spirit of the living Lord" (p. 276). Nevertheless, at most Rahner cautiously suggests here an analogy ("after the manner of") and certainly does not propose that the first disciples' experience of the risen Christ was simply "equivalent to other experiences of the Spirit" (Perkins, p. 198). In fact Rahner goes on to stress "the peculiar nature" of the apostles' Easter experience, "an experience which is strictly *sui generis*" (p. 277).

Before leaving Perkins's comments on the Easter appearances, I want to note her judgments about the words attributed to the risen Jesus and reflect more fully on one final item, her tentative explana-tion of "the early Christian development of the Son of Man tradition" (p. 83). First, even if she believes there may be some echoes of traditional material in what the risen Lord says in the Easter narra-tives of Matthew, Luke and John, she insists that the three evange-lists have extensively reworked their sources or simply composed the material themselves (see, for example, pp. 135, 159, 163, 175, 178). Nowhere does she claim that any of the sayings derive from what the risen Jesus said on the occasion of the Easter encounters. Fuller argues that at least "the command to baptize was implicitly involved in the Risen One's appointment of apostles to proclaim the gospel" (p. 86). Yet, in general, he agrees that the community traditions and the theological interests of the evangelists helped to

shape the words placed on the lips of the risen Jesus by Matthew,
Luke and John (pp. 89–92, 105–06, 113, 154).

Apropos of the Son of Man traditions, Perkins suggests not only
that "the vision of the risen Jesus in Galilee" was "apparently interpreted through the Son of Man image," but even that the whole Son of
Man tradition may "have been tied to the tradition of a resurrection
vision of [=received by] Peter in Galilee" (p. 83). If the appearance of
Peter had this specific function in developing the Son of Man tradition, it is curious that the two (early) kerygmatic texts which report
this vision do not speak of the Son of Man but rather of "Christ" (1 Cor
15:3,5) or "the Lord" (Lk 24:34). Mk 16:7 seems to refer to an
appearance to Peter in Galilee. In that resurrection narrative Mark,
whatever sources he is using, does not talk of the Son of Man, but
simply of "Jesus of Nazareth, who was crucified" (Mk 16:6).

One should agree with Perkins that "the resurrection visions of
Jesus" were the "necessary catalyst" for the "Christian use" of the Son
of Man traditions (p. 83), at least in this general sense. Those
appearances were the necessary catalyst for the total existence of the
Christian community. Without them there would have been no
faith in the risen Jesus, no Christian movement and no Christian
traditions about Jesus in terms of the Son of Man or any other title
whatsoever. The question rather is: was there a special connection
between the resurrection appearances—in particular, the vision to
Peter in Galilee—and the early Christian development of the Son of
Man traditions? Some have argued that Mt 16:13–19 and 17:1–9
(where we do have the required items of the Son of Man, a [glorious]
appearance, Peter and Galilee) contain elements of an Easter vision
retrojected into the story of Jesus' ministry. But, as Perkins herself is
aware (p. 99), the evidence for this hypothesis is by no means
compelling. She is inclined to associate Mt 28:18–20 with the Son
of Man image in Dan 7:14 (p. 133). But the fact remains that
Matthew speaks here of "Jesus" (28:18) and not as such of the Son of
Man. Matthew uses the Son of Man image elsewhere, but here—to
say the least—does not introduce it explicitly.

The appearance traditions that we have tell heavily against Perkins' theory. They call the risen Jesus "Christ" (1 Cor 15:3; Gal 1:12; Lk 24:26,46), "Lord" (1 Cor 9:1; Lk 24:34; Jn 20 and 21, *passim*), "Son" (of God) (Gal 1:16) and often simply "Jesus" (for example, Lk 24:15; Mt 28;5,9,10,16,18; Jn 21:1; Acts 9:5). Only once (Lk 24:7) do we find in our appearance texts any reference to the Son of Man (and Galilee). If Perkins' suggestion is correct, one would have expected to find such material as "the Son of Man has risen indeed and has appeared unto Simon," or "I delivered to you what I also received, that the Son of Man died for our sins, that he was buried, that he was raised, and that he appeared to Cephas, and then to the twelve." In fact, there seems to be a notable lack of connection between the Son of Man tradition(s) and those of the appearances to Peter (in Galilee) or to anyone else. The dying Stephen sees "the heavens opened, and the Son of Man standing at the right hand of God" (Acts 7:56), but not even Luke reckons Stephen as a resurrection witness or this experience as an Easter appearance.

III

Our third author, Hans Kessler stresses the difficulty of knowing much about what happened on the occasion of the risen Christ's appearances (pp. 233–34, 335). Nevertheless, without having read either Fuller or Perkins, he endorses the same basic "description." (a) The divine activity freely initiated the risen Jesus' encounters with the disciples who were radically changed by these experiences (pp. 208–9, 215, 216, 235–36; see pp. 129, 149). Those encounters were (b) not events open to neutral observation (p. 220), but episodes of (Easter) revelation (p. 219) with deep (c) eschatological (pp. 304–07)[7] and (d) christological (pp. 311–67) significance. (e) The New Testament reports the conviction that the recipients of the appearances were commissioned and sent as witnesses (pp. 129, 130–31, 153). In reporting his encounter with the risen Jesus, Paul

uses the language of a prophetic vision which calls him to be the
apostle to the Gentiles (p. 154).

Kessler holds that the words of the risen Jesus in Matthew,
Luke and John are redactional—a view shared, as we have seen, by
Perkins and, in large part, by Fuller. The sayings of the risen Lord
express concepts and theological interests of the evangelists, and
reveal theological, ecclesiological, apologetic and missionary devel-
opments which came later in the history of the early Church (pp.
130, 233). Like Fuller (p. 166) and Perkins, Kessler does not agree
with the fairly common hypothesis that the transfiguration in Mk
9:2–8 (or Mt 17:1–9) is an Easter appearance story which has been
modified and retrojected into the ministry of Jesus (pp. 128–29, fn.
126).

Thus far I have pointed to reflections on the risen Jesus' appearances that are common to our three authors. There are clear differences as well. Unlike Fuller, Kessler will not use Acts as a pointer to
the "luminous" nature of Paul's encounter with the risen Jesus. Luke
presents this encounter as the story of a conversion effected through a
luminous appearance from heaven. But, as Kessler notes, the Damascus road story in Acts clearly differs from Paul's own version of the
story. Moreover, neither the early statements of the appearances (for
example, 1 Cor 15:5; Lk 24:34) nor the Gospel accounts of the
appearances use the terminology of light and conversion (Kessler, p.
157).

Kessler differs from Perkins by not toying with the view that
the Easter appearances could be understood as ecstatic experiences of
the Holy Spirit. He insists that Paul distinguishes between his
Easter experience (the last of a series according to 1 Cor 15:8) and his
later visionary and "spiritual" experiences. What Paul writes about
in 2 Cor 12:1–7, was *not* a repetition of the (last) Easter appearance
to him. Other New Testament authors and traditions likewise distinguish between (a) the appearances of the risen Christ, on the one
hand, and (b) the reception of the Holy Spirit and various later

ecstatic visions and experiences of the Spirit (Kessler, pp. 155–56). Very closely connected with this last point is an important difference between Perkins, on the one hand, and Kessler (and Fuller), on the other. The New Testament presents the Easter appearances as episodes that were limited to the origin of Christianity and not repeatable (*ibid.*). Kessler notes how the aorist tense of *ōphthē* (1 Cor 15:5,6,7,8) indicates a closed series of events (p. 152). He goes on to develop the unique quality of the original Easter experiences (pp. 254–56).

A final difference between Kessler and Perkins. Along with quite a few others, Perkins calls the Easter appearances "Christophanies." Kessler is reluctant to introduce that term, arguing that we are better off without it: "The hellenistic root '*phan*' belongs predominantly in the context of the cosmic-sacred or mythical-eternal presence of the Divine" (p. 233; see p. 228, fn. 259). Such a context does not correspond properly to the New Testament reports about the risen Christ's appearances.

Kessler's contribution to the discussion about the Easter appearances is twofold. First, he explores fairly thoroughly the possibility of the appearances of the risen Jesus having been imaginative, mystical visions produced by God (pp. 221–27). We noted above how Fuller, without explaining matters, simply affirms that "even" the language of "religious mysticism" cannot "categorize the Easter appearances" (p. 33). In his *Foundations of Christian Faith* (New York, 1978), Karl Rahner briefly discourages us from likening the disciples' Easter experiences "too closely to mystical visions of an imaginative kind," reported by later Christians (p. 276). An accurate "theology of myticism" does not recognize the visions of mystics as being on a par "with the appearances of the risen Christ to the apostles" (*ibid.*, p. 274). In her *Resurrection* Perkins draws on Rahner but not in this context. She does not reflect on possible analogies to be drawn from mysticism. Others, however, have done so. In his *The Idea of the Holy* (London, 1958) Rudolf Otto, for instance, proposes that "the experiences concerned with the Resurrection were *mystical experiences*" (p. 223), "spiritual experiences" that yielded "a mystical . . . apprehension of truth" (p. 226).

Kessler himself argues against seeking help from mysticism to illuminate the Easter encounters. Those experiences of the disciples depended very much on the divine initiative, and happened to them after the radical break in their lives brought by the crucifixion. Imaginative visions, however, depend more on the ongoing spiritual life of the mystics themselves. They are not the kind of "radically and qualitatively *new* intervention" of God that the Easter experiences were in the lives of the disciples (pp. 224–25). Kessler might have added that, unlike those Easter experiences, mystical experiences crop up constantly in the life of the Church. They are not restricted to the opening phase of Christianity, but, as Rahner observes in *Foundations of Christian Faith,* they can be reproduced and repeated "indefinitely" (p. 277). Furthermore genuine mystical experiences can be found outside the special story of Christianity. As an ongoing and general phenomenon of Christian and human religious life, mysticism can hardly be expected to illuminate much the Easter encounters which were reserved to a brief and special period of history.

Besides filling out Rahner's warning against comparing the Easter encounters too closely to the experiences of mystics, Kessler has the second merit of insisting on the unparalleled nature of the risen Jesus' appearances. He argues against using the common category of "visions" (pp. 223–29), and largely follows the austere Pauline lead of 1 Cor 15:5–8 and Gal 1:12, 16 by simply speaking of "appearances," "revelations" (pp. 233, 235). Here again Kessler successfully documents a brief claim made by Rahner: the Easter experience of the disciples was "strictly *sui generis*" (*Foundations of Christian Faith,* p. 277).

To conclude. We have to follow the austere Pauline lead (1 Cor 15:5–8; Gal 1:12, 16) and remain content with the spare description of the risen Christ's appearances offered by Fuller and endorsed by Perkins, Kessler and others. They converge, as we have seen, in holding several basic conclusions about those encounters. More precise definition of the appearances as luminous, ecstatic, "spiritual" or mystical experiences remains unsupported by the New Testament evidence.

It may seem frustrating that we can only make a few general statements about the form of the disciples' experience of the risen Christ. The specific nature of the appearances eludes us. Yet there is a vitally important lesson to be learned. The mysterious nature of the Easter appearances does nothing else than mirror the unique mystery behind them: the glorious resurrection of the crucified Jesus.

We have drawn little from the Gospels and the Easter stories of Matthew, Luke and John. Their narratives also mirror the mysterious, elusive quality of the appearances of the risen Lord. Behind closed doors, along a road, outside his open and empty tomb, on the shores of a lake, Jesus was simply there—to be recognized with astonished and reticent love: "It is the Lord" (Jn 21:7).

CHAPTER 2

Mary Magdalene as Major Witness to Jesus' Resurrection

The title of this chapter demands a definition of terms. Though most readers will immediately recognize Mary Magdalene as an historical person, and some may still (wrongly) identify her with "the woman who was a sinner" (Lk 7:37), nevertheless the terms "major witness" and "resurrection" are often understood in diverse ways by different persons. Indeed, in first-century Judaism women were not qualified to testify in trials as witnesses.[1] ("From women let no evidence be accepted, because of the levity and temerity of their sex; neither let slaves bear witness . . ."[2]). Thus, if "witness" were applied to Mary Magdalene in the legal context of those times, the title of this article would involve a contradiction in terms. Some people consider "resurrection" to be merely an idea[3] or, at the other extreme, the simple resuscitation of a corpse rather than the new, transformed life for a unique person, Jesus Christ.

The fact that some women, and Mary Magdalene in particular, were cited by the New Testament as witnesses for the resurrection, evoked scorn from those who opposed early Christianity. Origen needed to refute the charge that belief in the risen Jesus was based on the testimony of a "hysterical female," and "perhaps by someone else" (Peter?).[4] In various forms this prejudice against accepting women as witnesses has continued through the centuries. For instance, Ernest Renan built up Mary Magdalene as *the* (hallucinated) witness, whose love made her imagine that Jesus was personally risen and whose testimony convinced the other disciples.[5]

The early "witnesses" of the risen Jesus were the ones who got Christianity going. We know much about some and almost nothing about others. We have enough data to write books about Peter and Paul, yet we possess very few historical facts about Mary Magdalene. That only adds to the confusion and controversy. This lack of knowledge does not diminish her importance but demands that we rightly interpret it. She was great enough for Pope Leo the Great, soon after the Council of Chalcedon, to call her a "figure of the Church" (". . . *Maria Magadalene personam Ecclesiae gerens* . . ."),[6] and, a century later, for Pope Gregory the Great to refer to her as another Eve who announces not death but life.[7] Even before them, in the third century, Hippolytus of Rome referred to the women at the tomb of Jesus as "apostles,"[8] which developed into Mary Magdalene often being called the *apostola apostolorum.* Yet others like Celsus, Renan, and in our own time even a staunchly orthodox writer like Ricciotti[9] have downplayed her importance.

For the purposes of this article we will define "witness" as someone who has first-hand knowledge of facts or events. A major witness is one whose testimony is of greatest importance and/or is the most complete. By "resurrection" we mean the unique act by which God transformed and raised forever the person Jesus to his right hand (cf. Gal 1:1; "Paul, an apostle . . . through Jesus Christ and God the Father, who raised him from the dead" [RSV]). The primary and immediate evidence on which the witnesses relied to assert this came from (1) appearances to them of the risen and transformed Jesus and (2) their discovery of the empty tomb. These appearances had a profound, transforming effect on the lives of those who had known and been associated with Jesus during his brief life on this planet.

New Testament Data

To analyze Mary Magdalene's role as major witness to the resurrection, let us begin by examining the New Testament data. Joseph Fitzmyer, in the second volume of his commentary on Luke's Gospel, lists and describes the six resurrection narratives which are found in the Gospel tradition:

1. Mark 16:1–8. The discovery of the empty tomb by the women (Mary Magdalene, Mary the mother of James, and Salome). A "young man" charges them to go and tell the disciples and Peter that Jesus goes before them to Galilee, where they will see him. The women flee and say nothing to anyone, "for they are afraid." There are no appearances of the risen Christ.

2. Matthew 28:1–20. The discovery of an empty tomb by two women (Mary Magdalene and another Mary). An angel and then Jesus appears to them, and Jesus tells them to break the news to the others. Later on, the risen Christ appears to the eleven in Galilee and commissions them to make disciples, to teach and to baptize.

3. Luke 23:56b–24:53. This narrative consists of five episodes: (a) the finding of the empty tomb by the women (Mary Magdalene, Mary the mother of James, Joanna, and others); they are told by the two men in gleaming robes to recall the words Jesus had addressed to them while he was still in Galilee; the women leave and report it all to the eleven, who regard their stories as so much nonsense; Peter alone goes off to see for himself (and then the risen Christ appears to him). (b) The risen Christ appears to the disciples on the road to Emmaus; (c) Christ appears to the eleven and their companions in Jerusalem; (d) he commissions them to be "witnesses of this" and to preach in his name; and (e) he leads them out to Bethany, where he parts from them and is carried off to heaven on Easter Sunday night.

4. John 20:1–29. The discovery of the empty tomb by Mary Magdalene, who tells Simon Peter and the beloved disciple. This is followed by the appearance of the risen Christ to Mary, his appearance to disciples in Jerusalem on Easter Sunday evening, with Thomas absent, and his appearance a week later, with Thomas present.

5. John 21:1–23 (the appendix to the Johannine Gospel). The risen Christ appears to seven disciples who have been fishing on the Sea of Tiberias, after which Simon Peter is commissioned to feed Christ's sheep. This section presents the contrasting roles of Peter and the beloved disciple.

6. Mark 16:9–20 (the Marcan appendix). Three appearances in the Jerusalem area on the first day of the week. The first of these is to Mary Magdalene; the second is to two disciples walking into the country, who go back and report it to disbelieving disciples; the third is to the eleven, whom Christ upbraids for disbelief and finally commissions to preach the Gospel to all creation. Christ is then taken up into heaven, seated at the right hand of God, and the disciples go forth to preach.[10]

What should strike the reader of this schematic presentation is the fact that Mary Magdalene is mentioned in five out of the six Gospel narratives and, when mentioned, is always the first person named. Is this merely accidental or were the Gospel writers recognizing her importance? Fitzmyer (apropos of point 3 above) notes that reference is first made to some women of Galilee even though their testimony does not engender faith and is even discredited by the apostles (p. 1543). Raymond Brown, in his comments on Jn 20:10 (point 4 above), says: "The real purpose of this verse is to get the disciples off the scene and give the stage to Magdalene."[11]

In these six Gospel narratives Peter is mentioned by name in four (1, 3, 4, 5 above) and is spoken of together with Mary Magdalene in three (1, 3, 4). Peter is not mentioned in Matthew 28, the chapter which announces both the resurrection and the post-resurrection command to evangelize the world.

Interpretation of the Data

We have recalled the basic New Testament data about Mary Magdalene as Easter witness. What do exegetes and theologians make of that data?

Rudolf Bultmann compares the account of the Easter appearances as found in John 20 with those of the Synoptic Gospels. He
notes that in John's account Mary Magdalene recognizes the risen
Christ when he calls her by name. Bultmann points to the meaning
which this narrative undoubtedly has: ". . . the shepherd knows his
sheep and 'calls them by name' (Jn 10:3), and when they hear his
voice they recognize him. Perhaps we may also add: the naming of
the name tells a man what he is; and to be known in such a way leads
a man to the encounter with the Revealer."[12] Bultmann qualifies this
by saying that Mary Magdalene cannot enter into fellowship with
Christ until she has recognized him as the Lord who is with the
Father (p. 687). Her message to the disciples is the core of Easter
faith: understanding the offense of the cross (p. 688). In contrast to
Luke's account, nothing is said about the impression her message
makes on the disciples (p. 689).

Edwyn Hoskyns also speaks of the shepherd-sheep image[13] and
believes that the message which Mary Magdalene had to deliver to
the disciples was "that the new order, the order of the powerful
action of the Spirit of God, the New Covenant, was now imminent"
(p. 543). He points out that while in the three Synoptic Gospels
Mary Magdalene is the first woman named in the Easter texts, in the
Fourth Gospel "the emphasis rests entirely upon the appearance of
the Lord to Mary and upon the words which he addressed to her"
(ibid.).

C.H. Dodd compares the post-resurrection scenes in the Gospels and then evaluates them. He considers Matthew 28 to mean
that Christ comes in glory to reign over all.[14] He believes that for
Luke the appearances have evidential value: the apostles know that
the Lord is alive and will come again (ibid.). John's Gospel presents the appearances as the renewal of Jesus' personal relations
with the apostles. The appearances help to consolidate the renewed contact (pp. 442–43). Dodd thus passes over the women's
significance.

C.K. Barrett takes John 20 to be dependent on the older tradition of 1 Cor 15:5—8 and Mk 16:1—8.[15] In that older tradition nothing is said of an appearance to Mary Magdalene. Barrett believes that John 20 intends to give the central place to the beloved disciple (*ibid.*). This, of course, reduces the significance of the women to almost nothing.

Though women, and in particular Mary Magdalene, were chronologically the first to encounter the risen Christ according to John, Matthew and the Marcan appendix, does that make them the major or even the most important witnesses of the resurrection? In the oldest account of the post-resurrection appearances St. Paul writes that "[Christ] appeared to Cephas, then to the Twelve. Then he appeared to more than five hundred brethren at one time, most of whom are still alive, though some have fallen asleep. Then he appeared to James, then to all the apostles. Last of all, as to one untimely born, he appeared also to me" (1 Cor 15:5—8 [RSV]). No specific mention of women as witnesses to the resurrection is found here (nor elsewhere in the New Testament except for the Gospels), and a priority of importance and time seems to be given to Cephas. Bernard, commenting on this passage in the International Critical Commentary, notes the absence of any reference to Mary Magdalene and asserts that the Church's faith in the resurrection is based on the appearances to the leaders of the future Church (Peter and James).[16]

Are the resurrection appearances (and those who witnessed to them) a necessary part of the Easter faith? Were they part of the early Church preaching of the Easter faith? Hans Kessler, in his recent book on the resurrection, acknowledges the importance of the appearances but spends most of his time on the Pauline material rather than on the Gospel accounts.[17] William Thompson notes how some have argued that these appearances were neither necessary for faith nor always part of the early preaching:

> Koester and Schillebeeckx build a somewhat strong case on the
> fact that there are apparently quite early kerygmata which do

not mention Jesus' death and resurrection. Jesus is proclaimed, in these, as (1) the coming Lord of the future (1 Cor 16:22; Rev 22:20; 1 Cor 15:51–52; Lk 17:24), as (2) the divine miracle worker (Acts 2:22; 2 Cor 3:1; 5:12; 4:5) as (3) Holy Wisdom's envoy/Wisdom itself (Lk 11:49–51; Mt 11:27; Phil 2:6–11; Jn 1:1–16). [18]

Yet, if we ask ourselves whether the post-resurrection appearances are necessary to resurrection belief, we must keep in mind 1 Cor 15:5–8 and Lk 24:34, where they are considered essential. Thompson himself opts for the death-resurrection model (and the importance of the appearance tradition) because the New Testament and later Christianity prefer this model over others (p. 223). After he points out that some biblical scholars reconstruct the historical evidence without pursuing the possible meaning of resurrection in our experience, Thompson urges the student to complement historical research with a more philosophical-theological form of analysis which tries to tackle experiential questions. He adds that "some theologians needlessly ignore the possibility of exploring possible experiential correlates to the resurrection belief, thus passing over its significance for us today" (p. 227). [19]

Thompson finds an example of such an "experiential correlate" in the fact that a person can continue to keep on trusting after the death of a loved one (a "foretaste" of resurrection in our own experience). Another example which he gives is a person's experience of passing from ignorance, bias and bigotry to greater insight, less bias, and more openness as a kind of death-resurrection passage (p. 228).

Thompson believes that the striking role of women in the resurrection texts is a strong tradition which contains an important lesson for us (p. 232). He recalls the view endorsed by some biblical scholars that women were only unofficial witnesses of the resurrection, while the "real" witnesses were the male disciples, especially Peter. In fact, in some texts Peter enjoys a primary role as witness (1

Cor 15:5; Lk 24:34; Mk 16:7; Jn 20:1–10). But, Thompson continues, "The point is still secure: in the tradition women are the first
witnesses, regardless of any role that Peter may play or may have
come to play in the Church" (p. 232).[20]

When Rudolf Schnackenburg comments on John's Gospel,[21]
especially John 20, he notes that the events on the morning of Easter
Sunday are held together as one whole through Mary Magdalene (p.
301). John's concentration on Mary Magdalene is not surprising,
because of his tendency to bring individual persons to the fore (p.
305). Schnackenburg believes that the choice of Mary Magdalene as
a messenger of the Risen One is not the creation of the fourth
evangelist but taken over from his source (p. 308). He adds that
Mary's encounter with the Risen One "represents for the evangelist
the climax which, according to his Christological thought, he emphasizes strongly" (p. 315).

In the end, however, Schnackenburg does what Ricciotti and
others do: he subordinates the testimony of women to that of the
male disciples. He uses Luke rather than Paul to establish the case:

> The reference to the oldest list of appearances in 1 Cor 15:5–8,
> in which such a Christophany to Mary Magdalene, or still more
> women is lacking, is, admittedly, no serious counter-argument,
> because the primitive Church obviously did not place any value
> on the testimony of women; but Luke's silence carries weight
> because he does assign a certain role to the women, but does not
> know of an appearance by Jesus to them (cf. 24:22–24). For
> John, the value of the story which he found is not on a historical
> but a theological level. In Mary's encounter with Jesus the
> meaning of Jesus' resurrection for the fellowship of the disciples
> finds expression; it forms a [mere?] prelude to Jesus' appearance
> before the disciples to whom the risen Lord gives the Spirit and
> grants authority (p. 321).

This argument from Luke contrasts with an explanation given a few
years earlier by Z.C. Hodges: "For Luke, the extended manifestation

to two male witnesses at once is the heart of his resurrection narrative and its effect is not to be diminished by even an allusion to prior female witnesses. Accordingly, the evangelist's silence [about the appearances to women] is due to a literary tendency."[22] Moreover, the claim that "the primitive Church obviously did not place any value on the testimony of women" is hardly compatible with the fact that all four Gospels report Jesus' tomb to have been found empty by one (John) or more (the Synoptics) women.

A middle course about women's testimony is that advocated by Hubert Ritt.[23] He believes that women are primarily associated with witnessing to the death of Jesus, but not to his resurrection. Their role is to focus attention on actions at the grave rather than on the Easter message.[24]

Women come to be mentioned in connection with the Easter message because two different narratives (Passion and Easter) are joined to form a literary unity. This is best seen in 1 Cor 15:3b–5, where in the kerygma of the early Church the death and burial of Jesus are briefly but clearly linked to his resurrection.[25] The New Testament accounts present women more as "addressees" of the Easter message than as witnesses.[26] The story of the women at the grave is connected with the Easter Gospel ("Jesus now lives in a totally different way"), but it is above all the twelve who guarantee the Easter Gospel.[27] Even Jn 20:2 does not show the women as witnesses of the Easter Gospel.[28] In fact, Mark tells us that the reactions of the women to the angel's message were anxiety, fear, silence and flight.[29] Ritt thus concludes that the women cannot be considered Easter witnesses since at most they give us only the message that Jesus had risen and not the full Easter Gospel.

A year after the article by Ritt was published, François Bovon wrote specifically on Mary Magdalene for *New Testament Studies*.[30] He points out that exegetes have often considered the appearance to Mary Magdalene among later, popular additions to the text ("tardifs et légendaires"—p. 51). He believes, however, that it is important to examine possible reasons for the appearances being included in the overall structure of a Gospel or epistle. Since Peter was the first leader of the Church, he is obviously mentioned in 1 Cor 15:5, as James and the other apostles are in 1 Cor 15:7. The fact that Mary Magdalene is mentioned at all shows that the early Church considered her important and intended to include her as a witness.[31] She has always been associated with Easter and the founding of the Church. Thus the Church has been careful to link her to the discovery of the empty tomb and mention her, a woman, as an authentic Easter witness.[32]

Yet how do we explain that Mary Magdalene is missing from the names provided by 1 Cor 15:5–8? Bovon asserts that the list of people given by Paul represents a compromise between the Judeo-Christianity of Jerusalem (represented by Peter and James) and that of the Hellenistic world (represented by Paul himself). This compromise was made at the expense of other groups such as the Johannine Church. To include Mary Magdalene in a kerygmatic list would alienate some groups for several reasons: (1) those people from a Jewish background would not accept a woman's testimony; (2) the Church was concentrating on setting up a ministry of males hostile to prophetic witness; (3) a woman would detract from Peter and Paul, whom the early Church was enphasizing.[33]

A scholar who from a feminist viewpoint has analyzed the role of women (and especially Mary Magdalene) as witnesses of the resurrection is Elizabeth Schüssler-Fiorenza.[34] She points out the continuity of fidelity in the female disciples who had stood with Jesus in his suffering, sought to honor him in his death, and then became proclaimers of his resurrection (p. 322). She relies on the work done by Raymond Brown (*The Community of the Beloved Disciple*) to assert that the discipleship and leadership of the Johannine community included both women and men, and that the " 'Johannine Christians, represented by the Beloved Disciple, clearly [regarded] themselves as closer to Jesus and more perceptive' than the churches who [claimed] Peter and the twelve as their apostolic authority" (p. 326).

Schüssler-Fiorenza recognizes two traditions which coexist side by side in the accounts of the post-resurrection appearances—the tradition of Mary Magdalene being the primary apostolic witness to the resurrection (Matthew, John and Marcan appendix), and the tradition of the Petrine primacy (Paul and Luke). She finds it remarkable that these two independent streams of the Gospel tradition have both survived (p. 332).[35] She points out that the role of women in the Church has always been the subject for much debate: patristic Christianity downplayed the significance of women, especially Mary Magdalene, as the primary witnesses of the resurrection, and highlighted figures like Peter, Paul and the twelve, whereas the non-canonical gospels claimed women disciples as apostolic authorities for the reception of revelation and secret teaching (pp. 304–05). Apocryphal writings of the second and third centuries which speak of the competition between Peter and Mary Magdalene reflect the tension that existed on the question of primacy of apostolic authority. In fact, the "argument between Peter and Mary Magdalene clearly reflects the debate in the early church on whether women are the legitimate transmitters of apostolic revelation and tradition" (p. 306).

Before we move on, let us make three more points about Schüssler-Fiorenza's position. Although she recognizes two post-resurrection traditions that coexist in the New Testament, she does not distinguish between them in the way that exegetes usually do: the appearances that took place in Galilee (presumably to Peter, the twelve, etc.) and those which occurred in and around Jerusalem (to Mary Magdalene, James, etc.). These post-resurrection appearances were thus separated according to where different groups happened to be present at a given time rather than by any distinction between male apostles and female believers. Second, early Church writers (e.g., Clement of Rome, Ignatius of Antioch, Justin Martyr, Irenaeus) are quite silent about any debate as to whether women can legitimately transmit apostolic revelation and tradition. (In fact, Clement goes out of his way to praise women like Esther and Judith for what they had done for their people; cf. 1 *Clem* 55.) Schüssler-Fiorenza herself admits it is (only) Gnostic and apocryphal writings which "claim women disciples as [separate?] apostolic authorities for the reception of revelation and secret teachings" (p. 304). These writings belong to the second and third centuries. She does not appreciate the importance of Mk 16:9–11, where Jesus is said to have appeared (chronologically) *first* to Mary Magdalene. Yet, in what follows (Mk 16:12–20) there is no suggestion of a conflict between Mary Magdalene and Peter as apostolic authorities. This important second-century addition to Mark's Gospel (16:9–20) knows Mary Magdalene's importance but fails to vindicate Schüssler-Fiorenza's thesis. We must ask ourselves, therefore, whether the Gnostics accurately preserve what was present from the beginning. Are they reliable guides or just a decadent spinoff?[36] Third, patristic Christianity at times downplayed the significance of women. Yet, as we saw, Leo the Great, Gregory the Great and others could pay remarkable tribute to the person of Mary Magdalene.

Schüssler-Fiorenza does not refer to Pheme Perkins' book *The Gnostic Dialogue,* published three years earlier, which challenges the reliability of the Gnostic writings as guides to the origin and development of Christianity. Perkins wrote at a time when Elaine Pagels had just popularized the Gnostic/orthodox conflict. According to Perkins, Pagels, in *The Gnostic Gospels,* was mistaken in portraying the Gnostics "as champions of individual creativity against an increasingly repressive and unimaginative orthodoxy."[37]

> She [Pagels] claims that gnosis represents the form in which Christian symbols continue to inspire great creative artists, otherwise alienated by a rigid orthodox Christianity. Gnostics insist on the rights of the autonomous, creative human self. The preceding section has already taken issue with the historical

inaccuracies in such presentations of the Gnostic/orthodox rela-
tionship. We have seen that Gnostics did not have the picture
of the autonomous, differentiated, creative self presupposed in
this argument. Such a view of the self is largely the product of
modern thought and presupposes a consciousness of self and
world radically different from that of second- and third-century
people (p. 205).

In a later work Perkins refers favorably to Elizabeth Schüssler-
Fiorenza's assertions that women were part of the larger group of
witnesses from which a successor to Judas was chosen, and that they
were also commissioned as missionaries.[38] Perkins, however, approaches her subject more from an exegetical point of view than from
one which attempts to recruit the early Christian story for the
purposes of a feminist theological reconstruction.[39]

When Perkins compares Matthew's account of the resurrection
(28:1–10) to that of Mark (16:1–8), she points out how the former
clarifies ambiguities found in the Marcan account (pp. 126–30).
Specifically, just as "Matthew made the figure at the tomb unmistakably an angel, so he attributes to the angel knowledge of the
women's errand. He shifts the announcement of resurrection to the
beginning of the angel's message. Thus he makes it clear that Jesus
is not in the tomb because he has been raised. With the earlier
apologetic emphasis on the posting of the guard at the tomb, there
can be no other explanation for the absence of Jesus' body" (p. 128).
Perkins then adds: "The priority of the message that Jesus has been
raised is also evident in the commission to the women. They are to
go quickly and announce that Jesus has risen. Thus, they are primarily messengers of the resurrection" (p. 129). She interprets Jesus'
words to the women, "Do not be afraid; go and tell my brethren to
go to Galilee and there they will see me" (Mt 28:10), as a command
that the women must carry out the commission they had received
from the angel.

Perkins' comments on Mt 28:16–20 contain her reflections on the role of Peter. After she points out that "and Peter" is missing from the angel's instructions to the women (though found in Mark's version), she says:

> Matthew gives Peter primacy in the gospel as spokesperson for the disciples, as guardian of Jesus' interpretation of the Law, and as representative of the typical disciple, but he does not place Peter above the others. He is firmly anchored within the circle of disciples to whom the ministry of the post-Easter church is entrusted. One might even wonder if some scholars have gone too far in pushing 1 Cor 15:5 to imply that the primacy that Peter enjoyed among the disciples was based on his rallying the others after his vision of the risen Lord (pp. 131–32).[40]

Perkins concludes her analysis of the resurrection accounts of Mark and Matthew by arguing that there are three sources of primitive resurrection traditions behind the Gospel narratives. They are (1) the old kerygmatic tradition that is reflected in 1 Cor 15:3–5, (2) that of the empty tomb found by the women disciples, and (3) that of the Christian prophets who speak in the name of the Lord, proclaiming his messianic exaltation (p. 137).

In her comments on Luke's resurrection accounts (24:36–49) Perkins says that the commission to witness is intended for the entire group of those who have followed Jesus from Galilee. That group explicitly includes a number of women disciples of Jesus, and so this commissioning is also meant for them (p. 167). She notes that in Lk 24:34 the phrase is used, "The Lord has risen indeed and appeared to Simon," while in Jn 20:18 Mary Magdalene says, "I have seen the Lord." Perkins believes that this deliberate replacement by John is an acknowledgment of Mary Magdalene's equality with Jesus' other disciples as a witness to the resurrection (p. 177).

Summary and Conclusions

Before we draw conclusions, we should summarize the data we have presented. To examine Mary Magdalene's role as the major witness of the resurrection, we began by defining our terms. Not only is a witness one who has first-hand knowledge of a certain set of facts, but a major witness is one whose testimony is of greater importance or the most complete. By resurrection we mean God's transformation of Jesus after his death to a new and glorified state. The immediate evidence on which the Easter witnesses relied came, after all, from Jesus' post-resurrection appearances to them and the discovery of his empty tomb.

To support our topic, we examined Fitzmyer's analysis of the Gospel evidence. He listed six resurrection narratives. Mary Magdalene is mentioned in five of the six. When mentioned, she is always the first person named. We also cited Brown, who noted that in Jn 20:10 the evangelist purposely arranged the material so that Mary Magdalene would have the stage.

The Gospels, however, are not the only scriptural evidence to be considered. The epistles of Paul are an earlier source, and in his longest account of the resurrection (1 Cor 15:3–8) not only is no mention made of women but the importance of Cephas as a recipient of a post-resurrection appearance is stressed. This would seem to be contrary to the evidence presented in the previous paragraph.

Various solutions have been offered to the above dilemma. Some examples are: (1) two traditions have survived, coexisting side by side; (2) two traditions have survived, one subordinate to the other (the Gospel accounts subordinate to that of Paul); (3) the appearances are not really a necessary part of the Easter faith, so why worry?

To further complicate the problem, we know that historically there was a prejudice against admitting women as witnesses. Not only did this prejudice exist at the time of Jesus, but even in the twentieth century biblical commentators have tended to stress that the basis of faith in the resurrection comes from the male apostles and not from the testimony of women. If appearances were admitted as evidence, then only those to the (male) apostles were considered in any way as normative.

An examination of some writings of the "classical" commentators on John—Bultmann, Hoskyns, Dodd and Barrett—showed quite diverse opinions about the meaning and importance of the post-resurrection appearances. Bultmann very positively considered Mary Magdalene to be the bearer of the core of the Easter faith, and Hoskyns portrayed her as the deliverer of the message that the new covenant was imminent. Dodd, however, was interested in the appearances but not the women, while Barrett believed that only the beloved disciple was important in John 20, *the* Gospel chapter in which Mary Magdalene is most completely described.

Prejudice against women has been rightly challenged in recent years. This is seen especially in issues brought up by the feminist movement. Such a challenge has had its effect on the interpretation of Scripture and forced a rethinking of "traditional" positions. The title of this article is an example in point. Until recently few authors would have asserted that Mary Magdalene should be considered a major witness of the resurrection.

Though it can be said that post-resurrection appearances are not as such the *object* of Easter faith, but rather the primary historical *catalyst* of it, nevertheless the Church has always recognized the essential importance of the appearance tradition. One who accepts this tradition should agree that women were the first or among the first witnesses. In this tradition women, especially Mary Magdalene, have a lead role. Above all, in John 20 Mary Magdalene is the human figure who holds the events together.

A question arises as to whether the appearance tradition which includes women (Gospels) is as important as that of the male leaders in the early Church (1 Cor 15). To the extent that we admit the evidence from Gnostic and apocryphal writings of the second and third centuries, we will hold that even by then this question had not been satisfactorily resolved, since there was debate as to whether or not women were legitimate transmitters of revelation. By the sixth century, however, Pope Gregory the Great spoke of Mary Magdalene as being a new Eve who revealed life to males.

Rather than arguing for a priority of importance among the traditions, Pheme Perkins talks about the differences between them. This does not mean they are contradictory. After examining the New Testament evidence, she concludes that Peter is (1) the spokesperson for the disciples, (2) guardian of Jesus' interpretation of the law, (3) representative of the typical disciple but not above the others, (4) part of the group in charge of the post-Easter ministry of the Church (this last function not being based on any appearances). The women were (1) the primary messengers who were commanded to announce the resurrection, and (2) among those commissioned to witness. In addition, Mary Magdalene was considered equal to a (male) disciple as a witness for the resurrection.

This synthesis does not deny authority to Peter, nor does it ignore the fact that he was the recipient of a post-resurrection appearance. It does, however, show the complementary roles of women, Peter, and the other disciples as witnesses to the risen Christ. Among the female recipients of the appearances, Mary Magdalene is portrayed in Scripture as having the primary role.

CHAPTER 3

Did Jesus Eat the Fish?
(Luke 24:42–43)

The highpoint of Luke's realistic presentation of the Easter appearances comes when the risen Jesus asks his disciples for something to eat. "They gave him a piece of boiled fish, and he took it and ate before them" (Lk 24:42–43). The passage is echoed twice in the Acts of the Apostles. While "eating with" (Acts 1:4)[1] the apostles, the risen Jesus commanded them to wait in Jerusalem for the coming of the Holy Spirit. During his meeting in Caesarea with Cornelius, Peter testified to Jesus' resurrection in these terms:

> God raised him on the third day and made him manifest, not to all the people but to us who were chosen by God as witnesses, who ate and drank with him after he rose from the dead (Acts 10:40–41)

In Lk 24:43 only Jesus eats but he does not drink.[2] In Acts the disciples also eat with him (Acts 1:4) and they drink as well (Acts 10:41).

When the risen Jesus appeared to the disciples did he eat and drink (stage one of the tradition)? What place could such a motif of post-resurrection eating with the disciples have had in the life of the early Church (stage two of the tradition)? Where do we see the conscious intentions of Luke at work in this talk about eating (and drinking) in the post-resurrection situation (stage three of the tradition)? In answering these questions and interpreting Lk 24:43, we can also observe and report how various exegetes think it appropriate to introduce a similar Easter tradition from another Gospel (Jn 21:9–14), corrective material from Paul (canonical criticism), theological questions about Jesus' new state (can a risen body digest food and grow?), and reflections which go beyond what the evangelist Luke meant to what the episode might mean today (actualizing hermeneutics).

Stage One of the Tradition

In *The Gospel According to Luke X–XXIV*[3] J.A. Fitzmyer judges Jesus' request for food and eating the fish in front of his disciples to be "Lukan embellishments" (p. 1574) which belong to stage three of the tradition (p. 1576). With Luke several other New Testament authors attest reliably stage one of the tradition: the risen Jesus appeared to the disciples when they were gathered together (1 Cor 15:5ff; Lk 24:36; Mt 28:16ff; Jn 20:19). But when Luke has Jesus eating fish, he is "indulging" a "sort of realism" which sets him apart from the other evangelists (Fitzmyer, p. 1577). In reaching this conclusion, Fitzmyer will not, however, appeal to Paul's reflections on the risen body (above all, 1 Cor 6:12 ff; 15:42ff) which might create problems for Luke's realistic presentation of the post-resurrection Jesus.

Some contemporary exegetes maintain that the risen Jesus' eating with his disciples goes back to stage one of the tradition and the post-Easter events themselves. Thus I.H. Marshall in *The Gospel of Luke*[4] argues that in 24:43 Luke is using an historically reliable, "well-attested tradition." In support of his position Marshall points to Jn 21:13 and Acts 1:4; 10:41 (p. 903). This of course, is to slip over the fact that in Acts 1:4 and 10:41 it is the same author referring back to what he had already written in his first work. As we shall see, in the two subsequent passages he is qualifying or correcting what he had written in Lk 24:43. In Jn 21:13 it is by no means clear that Jesus himself eats: "Jesus came and took the bread and gave it to them, and so with the fish."

Marshall faces two difficulties, one historical and the other theological. He points to the "indisputable" evidence that "fish was readily available in Jerusalem" (p. 903), and so could have been eaten there by the disciples and the risen Jesus. More importantly, Marshall realizes that Luke's emphasis on "the physical reality" of Jesus' resurrection body

> leads to an apparent contradiction with Paul's dictum that "flesh and blood shall not inherit the kingdom of God" and his insistence on the spiritual nature of the resurrection body, but the conflict is apparent rather than real. Paul is concerned with the nature of the body in the new life after the resurrection of the dead in the kingdom of God, while Luke is concerned with the appropriate form of the manifestation of the risen Jesus in earthly conditions, and his narrative makes it plain that although Jesus has flesh and bones, he is able to appear and vanish in a way that is not possible for ordinary men. Both writers agree that resurrection is concerned with the body and not with a bodiless soul or spirit (pp. 900–01).

All the same, some difficulties remain. Did "the appropriate form of manifestation of the risen Jesus in earthly conditions" include *really* eating (and digesting) food? If so, can this be reconciled with Paul's teaching that in the risen life eating and the work of the stomach will be set aside (1 Cor 6:13)? Or did the risen Jesus merely pretend to eat?

From an earlier generation Plummer, who like Marshall understands Luke to be reporting an historically reliable tradition in 24:42–43, shows himself aware of the objection of play-acting:

> The objection that, if Jesus took food in order to convince them [the disciples] that he was no mere spirit, when the food was not necessary for the resurrection-body, he was acting deceitfully, does not hold. The alternative "either a ghost, or an ordinary body needing food" is false. There is a third possibility: a glorified body capable of receiving food. Is there any deceit in taking food, which one does not want, in order to place others, who are needing it, at their ease? (p. 560).

Even if St. Paul is not explicitly mentioned here, one senses the pressure of the apostle's reflections on the risen state. Not everyone will be content with Plummer's version of a glorified body which neither needs nor wants food but yet is "capable of receiving" (and digesting?) it. Eating something to put others "at their ease" is an act of ordinary human courtesy. To attribute such motivation to the risen Jesus, however, risks banalizing the whole scene and picturing him as a kind of "resurrected gentleman."

At this point one could list the exegetes who take a position for or against the historicity of the fish episode in Lk 24:42–43. In *The Gospel According to Luke*,[5] L. Morris is perfectly clear about what happened: "Jesus dispelled their unbelief by calling for some food which he proceeded to eat" (p. 342). In his *Commentary on the Book of Acts*,[6] F.F. Bruce takes *sunalizomenos* in Acts 1:4 to mean "eating with," notes the reference to Lk 24:42–43 and Acts 10:41, and comments:

> Many Christians find it difficult to accept such statements as literally true. Plainly the resurrection body of our Lord had no need of material food and drink for its sustenance. . . . But why may He not have taken food in the company of His disciples, not for any personal need of his own, but in order to convince them that He was really present with them and that they were seeing no phantom? (p. 36)

No less than Marshall, Plummer and Morris, Bruce must face the questions: What happened to the food taken by the risen Jesus? Can a risen body digest food and grow?

This brief examination of views on stage one of the tradition can very well suggest that the end (stage three of the tradition) is where we appropriately start. We should investigate what we actually have, the text of the evangelist, reflect on Luke's intentions and literary product, and move back from there to stages two and one.

Stage Three of the Tradition

The fish episode falls within one literary unit (24:36—53), a section which recounts "but one appearance of the risen Christ" (Fitzmyer, p. 1573).[7] Within this larger literary unit, 24:36—43 serves as a prologue to what is to come in 24:44—53. Although Luke does not begin this section of his story by explicitly portraying the disciples at table in a meal-setting, the reader is meant to suppose that (Fitzmyer, p. 1574). Fitzmyer may be pressing Luke's narrative intention too far when he takes Jesus' question "Have you anything here to eat"? to mean: "Do you still have anything here to eat, anything left over from your evening meal"? (pp. 1576—77). It is one thing to recognize a meal setting for Luke's story. It is quite another thing to claim that the evangelist wants his readers to imagine that Jesus appears when the meal has ended.

At all events Luke's "apologetic motif" (Fitzmyer, p. 1574) is clear. In asking for something to eat and consuming it in their sight, the risen Jesus establishes his "physical reality" (Fitzmyer, p. 1575). Grundmann also notes Luke's "apologetical" purpose: "the bodiliness of the resurrection in the sense of the 'resurrection of the flesh' must be secured." Eating the fish proves bodily resurrection in a way that "brushes aside every doubt." The "apologetical meaning of the fish" is clear: "the bodily resurrection is so real that the Risen One can eat" (pp. 449, 451). J. Ernst identifies Luke's primary concern in similar terms: "someone who takes nourishment cannot be a ghost"; "any doubt about the bodily resurrection is excluded" when Jesus takes and eats food before the eyes of his disciples.[8]

One should add, however, that in the Jewish tradition eating would not necessarily indicate human bodiliness, whether risen or otherwise (see, for example, Gen 19:1–4; and the mission of Raphael in Tob 3:16–12:22). In the Book of Tobit the angel explains that he has not really been eating: "All these days I merely appeared to you and did not eat or drink, but you were seeing a vision" (Tob 12:19). Nevertheless, Luke's Gentile readers would presumably hold that spirits and angels do not eat and hence be satisfied that eating the fish establishes the risen Jesus' real bodiliness.

Behind the apologetic motif one can reasonably suppose two movements which the evangelist wishes to combat when writing his Gospel in the seventies or eighties. On the one hand, Luke could be answering those within the Christian community who over-spiritualize the resurrection or even deny it while maintaining the continuing, personal existence of Jesus' spirit. On the other hand, the evangelist may be also responding to outside critics who reject *tout court* that Jesus appeared as bodily risen from the dead and allege that the disciples experienced some ghostly phantom or even a mere figment of their imagination.

In this connection some exegetes speak of an "anti-docetic" concern which Luke shares in common with John (Ernst, pp. 666–67; Grundmann, p. 449). Marshall rightly points out that "the narrative is not concerned to refute docetism in the proper sense of that term, since it is concerned with the nature of the risen Jesus and not with the [human] nature of the earthly Jesus" (p. 900). Strictly speaking, docetism was a tendency which considered the humanity, sufferings and death of the earthly Jesus to be apparent rather than real. One might defend Ernst, Grundmann and others by allowing them to use the terms "docetic" and "anti-docetic" in a broader sense which would include controversies about the state of the risen Jesus.

Even if they do not share that strongly realistic version of stage one of the tradition which Marshall, Plummer and others hold,

Ernst and Grundmann feel the need to deal with the tension between Luke's realistic presentation of the risen Jesus and Paul's reflections on the spiritual body in 1 Cor 15:35–53. Grundmann attributes the difference to basically different interests. Paul's statements are "Christologically determined" while Luke follows an "anti-docetic intention" (p. 449), a distinction which does not throw much light on the subject. Whether understood in the stricter or the broader sense, an "anti-docetic intention" takes up Christological issues that concern the earthly or the risen Jesus. Grundmann's distinction does not face the heart of the difficulty: can we reconcile Luke's very realistic portrayal of the risen Jesus with Paul's version of the spiritual body? Or should we go so far as to argue that Jesus' risen existence differs significantly from our (future) risen existence, so that whereas he did on one occasion eat (Luke), this will not be true of us (Paul)?

Ernst does better in explaining why such "strongly materialistic elements" in Luke's account as Jesus' invitation to touch him (24:39) and his eating the fish (24:43) do not contradict Paul's statements on risen life and bodiliness. Luke is not offering a "realistic description" but rather "helps to interpretation" (p. 666). Ernst does not enlarge on what such "helps to interpretation" might be. Let me return to these shortly.

The Making of Luke 24:42–43

What lay behind the intimate and vivid scene of Luke 24:42–43? What elements from stage one and stage two of the tradition are particularly relevant for grasping the evangelist's intention?

I suggest that five items converged in the making of Luke's narrative: (a) a memory of the feeding of the five thousand with loaves and *fishes* (Mk 6:32–44 par), (b) the Last Supper (1 Cor 11:23–26 par), (c) an appearance of the risen Christ to the disciples when they were gathered together (1 Cor 15:5,7; Mt 28:16–20; Lk 24:36–53; Jn 20:19–23,26–29; 21:1–23; Mk 16:14–18), (d) a memory of initial doubts on the occasion of that appearance (Mt

28:17; Lk 24:36–41; Jn 20:24–25), and (e) the celebration of the Eucharist in the early community (see for example 1 Cor 11:23–26; Acts 2:42,46).

Together with these five elements we need to take into account two features of Luke's style: (i) a use at times of an imaginative, elaborated narrative, and (ii) a corrective self-commentary. Let us look at these two features in turn.

(i) Unlike the simpler statements from Jn 20:22–23 and Rom 5:5 about the gift of the Holy Spirit, Luke has an elaborate scenario for the day of Pentecost (Acts 2). We can find another example of (i) by setting Matthew's brief assertion about Mary being "found to be with child by the Holy Spirit" (Mt 1:18) alongside Luke's annunciation story (Lk 1:26–38). Both Matthew and Luke use a pre-Gospel "annunciation of birth" tradition (involving virginal conception through the Holy Spirit), but then Luke's story is more elaborated. In general, a certain freedom to adapt and embellish shows up more strongly in the first two chapters and last chapter of Luke (for example, in the Emmaus story)—a freedom which is comparable with his promise to provide authentic information about the story of Jesus and the origins of the Church (Lk 1:1–4; Acts 1:1–2). Luke does not misleadingly create important episodes *ex nihilo,* but on occasions he takes an historically reliable tradition (for example, the memory of an appearance to Cleopas and his companion) and writes it up in an elaborate way. In *Die Himmelfahrt Jesu* (Münich, 1971) Gerhard Lohfink finds the initial key to this descriptive art of Luke in the remark that at the baptism the Holy Spirit descended on Jesus "in bodily form" (Lk 3:22). Luke likes to present matters in a visible and tangible way (p. 247).

(ii) At times Luke deals more than once with the same material, qualifying and correcting an excessive realism that one passage alone could suggest. Thus the simpler account of Jesus' parting from his disciples on Easter day itself (Lk 24:50–51) offsets the vivid narrative of Acts 1:6–11. The promise of the Holy Spirit (Lk 24:49; Acts 1:4–5,8) puts matters in a less spectacular way than the richly embellished version of the day of Pentecost (Acts 2). In these cases the simpler versions forewarn the reader not to interpret in a wooden literalistic way the stories of the ascension and coming of the Spirit provided by Acts. Luke's self-correcting technique may also run in the opposite direction. Later material can qualify and correct what the reader has been given earlier. As we shall see, Acts 1:4 and, especially, Acts 10:41 work like that, qualifying and correcting the excessive realism of Lk 24:42–43.[9] One might argue that Acts 1:4 and, especially, Acts 10:41 simply presuppose the data furnished by Lk 24:42–43 and expand it, rather than correcting it. Where Lk 24:42–44 states that Jesus himself ate, Acts 10:41 adds that the disciples also ate and drank with him. However, such an argument ignores Luke's general technique of *corrective* self-commentary.

Luke's Message

It seems that Luke has three or four things to say through the fish-eating motif taken within its immediate literary context (24:36–53). First, this motif obviously aims at establishing the bodily reality of the resurrection and of the risen Lord's personal and living presence to his disciples (Ernst, Fitzmyer, Grundmann, Marshall, etc.). Luke knows of those who, both inside and outside the early Christian community, doubt or deny the bodily resurrection of Jesus. These doubters and opponents were anticipated by the disciples in Jerusalem who "disbelieved" their senses and wrongly "supposed that they had seen a spirit" when the risen Jesus stood among them. He finally removed their doubts and they recognized his bodily presence among them (Lk 24:36–43).

The bodily reality of the risen Jesus is stressed. At the same time, the corrective self-commentary provided by *Luke himself* speaks against taking the fish-eating motif literalistically.[10] If "twentieth-century readers" noticed this Lukan self-commentary they would not do what Fitzmyer hears them doing: "Only Luke among the evangelists indulges in this sort of realism about the existence of the risen Christ (who eats fish); and for this he is castigated by twentieth-century readers" (p. 1577). Luke mitigates the excessive realism of 24:42–43 first in Acts 1:4, where apostles "eat" with or simply "stay" with the risen Jesus. Acts 10:41 does not speak of Jesus himself eating but of the apostles eating and drinking in his company after the resurrection.[11] Thus the two passages in Acts comment on and qualify the heavy realism in Luke 24:42–43.

Luke seems to have received an old tradition of Christ appearing to his disciples on the occasion of a meal. He uses the tradition in different ways and for different purposes. In 24:36–43 he insists that Jesus was no mere ghost or phantom substitute but the same person now bodily risen and present to them. In Acts 1:4 the same tradition does not have such a strong apologetical intention but rather expresses "la familiarité ou la communauté de vie entre le Ressuscité et les disciples."[12] In Acts 10:41 the meal tradition serves to underline the qualifications of the apostles as valid witnesses to Jesus' resurrection.[13] Doubtless Luke here wants the reader to recall the two "meals" mentioned in the final chapter of his Gospel (24:30–31,35,41–43).

Luke and John 21 (see also Mk 16:14) share a common Easter tradition of table-fellowship involving the risen Lord, but (generally) use it differently in different contexts. Fish is very prominent in the Johannine version (Jn 21:3,5,6,8,9,10,11,13). Both in his Gospel and in Acts, Luke picks up this tradition and employs it, as we have seen, in a variety of ways. He brings in fish only once (24:42–43), but—as we shall see—like Jn 21:1–14 he also uses the tradition with eucharistic overtones.[14]

To sum up the primary significance of the fish-eating motif. It conveys the bodily reality and true appearance of the risen Lord to his chosen body of witnesses. It signifies his genuine resurrection from the dead, with the "new life" and "great joy" which that entails.[15]

The fish-eating motif also plays its part in depicting the credentials of the apostolic community as authentic witnesses to the resurrection. Cleopas and his companion first receive an interpretation of the Scripture before recognizing the risen Lord (Lk 24:31,35). It is an opposite sequence with the eleven apostles and the others in the Jerusalem community. They first see the risen Jesus (Lk 24:36–43), and then have their minds open to understand the Scriptures fulfilled in his resurrection from the dead (Lk 24:44–47). The evidence of their senses and a new insight into the Scriptures make them fundamental, universal witnesses (Lk 24:47–48).

Thus the fish-eating motif also functions to illustrate the origin and authenticity of the apostolic witness to the risen Jesus and mission in his name. The disciples can witness to him and begin their mission to the world because they have been with him during his ministry (Acts 1:21), have seen him "before them" (Lk 24:43) and now understand the deep meaning of the Scriptures. What took place "before them" when the risen Lord appeared constituted a special experience that made them normative witnesses to him and his resurrection from the dead.[16]

Besides figuring in a literary unit which expresses the apostles' qualifications as Easter witnesses, the fish-eating motif in Lk 24:42–43 has a third level of meaning. It fits into a broad pattern of meals in that Gospel: meals with Pharisees (7:36–50; 14:1–2), with sinners (19:1–10), the eschatological meal (12:37; 13:29), etc. In particular some literary correspondences link 24:42–43 ("fish," "he took it and ate") with the feeding of the five thousand in 9:16–17 ("taking the five loaves and the two fishes," "and all ate"), the passover meal in 22:19 ("he took bread") and the supper at Emmaus in 24:30 ("he took the bread"). As Guillaume states, the mention of fish in 24:42 "peut servir de renvoi aux poissons (9:16) de la multiplication des pains" and so refer (at least indirectly) to the Eucharist (p. 158, fn. 1). To be sure, Luke's eucharistic vocabulary and meaning come through more clearly in the "breaking of the bread" at Emmaus (24:30,35). But they are also present, albeit more discreetly, in what one might call "the breaking of the fish" in Jerusalem. Ernst

(p. 668) argues that the nature of the food in 24:42–43 (fish) is insignificant, but this is to miss the reference to the multiplication of the loaves *and fish* in Lk 9:10–17—an episode with strong liturgical and eucharistic overtones.

One difficulty against recognizing a sacramental meaning in Lk 24:42–43 comes from the fact that it is Jesus who eats and he eats alone. But the literary correspondences (noted above) between these verses and earlier episodes in the Gospel that unmistakably express eucharistic meaning encourage one to recognize also here a sacramental reference. Add too the eucharistic reference which also seems to be present when Luke takes up again the theme of table-fellowship with the risen Lord in Acts 1:4 and 10:41.[17] Since the related material which precedes and follows the passage has eucharistic overtones it appears plausible to acknowledge such overtones also in Luke 24:42–43.

In the fourth place, Luke's fish-eating motif could signify that the risen Jesus offers pardon to his followers who had abandoned and (in the case of Peter) denied him. In this Gospel, as elsewhere, eating together with Jesus expresses forgiveness of sins and reconciliation with God (see, for example, Lk 19:1–10). The problem about taking Lk 24:42–43 this way is twofold. Only Jesus himself is represented as eating; in the strict sense of the word there is no table-fellowship. More importantly, Luke has played down the disciples' need for repentance and a post-resurrection reconciliation. When Jesus is arrested, Luke does not add that the disciples "all fled" (Mk 14:50; Mt 26:56). After Peter's third denial, it is only in Luke's account that "the Lord turned and looked at Peter" (22:61)—a look expressing reproach and even more compassionate hope (see Lk 22:31–32). According to Luke, not only some female followers of Jesus but also "all his acquaintances" witnessed the crucifixion (23:49). Finally, Luke reports an appearance to Peter alone (24:34) which took place before the risen Jesus' encounter with the group. Thus Luke has reduced the need for post-Easter forgiveness to be expressed through renewed table-fellowship with Peter and the others. Possibly the fish-eating motif also symbolizes such reconciliation, but this meaning does not seem prominent in Luke's text and intentions.

In *Luke,* E. LaVerdière understands Lk 24:42–43 as an invitation to "the disciples and Luke's readers" "to extend nourishment to those in whom Jesus is really present." The passage "requires a commitment to the earthly lives of people"[18]—in the spirit of giving food to visiting strangers because the risen Lord identifies himself with them.

Perhaps this reflection works at the level of actualizing hermeneutics. But there is no evidence that through the fish-eating motif Luke himself had such a message in mind. It is through material concerned with the ministry of Jesus (Lk 16:19–31) or of his apostolic witnesses (for example, Acts 4:32–35) that Luke conveys the call to meet various needs in "the earthly lives of people."

To conclude. With other New Testament material Lk 24:42–43 recalls an appearance to the apostolic group on the occasion of their being together for a meal. But it does not follow that the risen Jesus quite literally ate (and drank) with his disciples (stage one of the tradition). In the life of the early Church (stage two of the tradition) a sacramental, eucharistic setting may have preserved the memory of the risen Lord's encounter with the disciples during their table-fellowship. Since it is an item shared by Lk 24:42–43 and Jn 21:1–14, fish may have figured in stage two of the tradition.

Luke himself (stage three of the tradition) uses the fish-eating actif as one of his means for expressing at least three things: (a) the bodily reality of the risen Lord, (b) the qualifications of the apostles as witnesses, and (c) the ongoing liturgical presence of the Lord. Possibly Lk 24:42–43 is also meant to communicate a sense of forgiveness and reconciliation. The main thrusts of the motif are apologetic (concerning the living Jesus himself), apostolic (concerning the normative witnesses to the resurrection) and sacramental (concerning the ongoing eucharistic life of the community). As part of his way of conveying these three points Luke employed the fish-eating motif. As we have seen, however, he does not want his readers to imagine that the risen Lord quite literally consumed (and digested) some fish before the astonished eyes of his disciples. The Christ who had already entered into his glory (Lk 24:26) was beyond all that.

CHAPTER 4

The Fearful Silence of Three Women (Mark 16:8c)

At least as we have it,[1] Mark's Gospel ends in an extraordinarily enigmatic fashion. It states that after discovering Jesus' tomb to be open and empty and hearing the angelic message about the resurrection and a coming rendezvous with the risen Jesus in Galilee, the three women fled in astonishment; "and they said nothing to anyone, for they were afraid" (Mk 16:8c).

This reaction on the part of Mary Magdalene, Mary the mother of James and Salome (Mk 16:1; see 15:40,47) has been somewhat prepared for when the text speaks of their being "amazed" (Mk 16:5–6) and of their flight from the tomb as trembling (*tromos*) and astonishment (*ekstasis*) came upon them (Mk 16:8a and b). Even so the final word about their fearful silence is surprising. Matthew seems to have been dissatisfied with what he found in Mark[2] and modifies the women's reaction: "they departed quickly from the tomb with fear *and great joy* and ran *to tell his disciples*" (Mt 28:8; see also Lk 24:9–10).

What are we to make of Mark's statement about the women's fearful silence? Is it to be understood in a more *historical* vein? Mark (or his source) knows the accounts of the empty tomb did not feature

53

in the early preaching of the resurrection (see 1 Cor 15:3b–5), and/
or that the women's story remained unknown for some time. He
acknowledges the fact that the story of the empty tomb only developed and/or entered the Easter message at a later stage by noting
that the women remained silent (= for some time did not publicly
speak about their empty tomb experience). Or does the three
women's fearful silence reveal a *theological* stance of the evangelist? In
that case his point could be negative (for example a disapproving
judgment against all Jesus' first disciples, both female and male) or
positive (for example, a picture of the appropriate, initial reaction to
the revelation of Jesus' resurrection). Here, of course, historical
concerns and theological interests overlap and are in no way understood to be mutually exclusive. Rather it is a matter of the predomi-
nant motive behind Mk 16:8c which could be of a more theological
or historical nature.

1. *An Historical Explanation*. Perhaps the most thoroughgoing
historical explanation of Mk 16:8c—and indeed of the whole
pericope, Mk 16:1–8—is that offered by Paul and Linda Badham in
Immortality or Extinction? (Totowa, N.J., 1982). According to them,
the evangelist himself created the whole of Mk 16:1–8: that is to
say, prior to the writing of this Gospel, there was simply no empty
tomb story at all. They interpret the Gospel's closing comment (Mk
16:8c) as implying

> that the empty tomb story formed no part of the generally
> received oral traditions about Jesus which circulated before the
> Gospels were written. It would be manifestly absurd for Mark
> to write that the women said nothing about it to anyone, if the
> story of their finding the empty tomb were generally known.
> The comment in fact only [sic] makes sense if Mark was con-
> scious that he was adding a new element to the generally
> received traditions about Jesus; an element which was not
> known prior to the publication of his Gospel, and which he

therefore had to account for by claiming that his sources had hitherto kept this knowledge secret out of fear.

In short "the story of the empty tomb was unknown before the appearance of Mark's Gospel" (pp. 23–24). The evangelist simply invented the whole story himself; his final words ("they said nothing to anyone, for they were afraid") show him trying to cover his tracks and hide from the reader the fact that "the generally received traditions about Jesus" contained no story about the discovery of the empty tomb.[3]

Yet would it have been "*manifestly absurd* for Mark to write that the women said nothing about it to anyone, if the story of their finding the empty tomb were generally known" (italics mine)? The conventions of *narrative* suggest that the women's silence should be understood as temporary: for the time being they did not deliver the message and tell others about what they had seen and heard. If Mark proposes their silence to have been permanent and absolute (= the women *never* said anything about their discovery to anyone whatsoever), what he writes would be "manifestly absurd." How could he, the narrator, know what the women had seen and heard if they quite literally never passed on their story to anyone?[4] The Badhams have confused "said nothing to anyone" with "never said anything to anyone whatsoever." Mark could quite reasonably write that the women "said nothing to anyone," even though the story of their finding the empty tomb was now generally known (at least in Jerusalem and the Holy Land).

The Badhams seem to be crediting Mark with the claim that his sources (= the three women or one or two survivors from the trio) had kept their knowledge of the empty tomb "secret out of fear" for thirty or forty years. The Christian message of Jesus' resurrection had long since spread around the Mediterranean world and there were growing Christian communities in most parts of the Roman empire. But Mark (implicitly) contends that three women remained afraid for decades and never broke their silence until they told him (in the middle or late sixties). Such a scenario about Mark and his alleged claim seems quite far-fetched. But this is what the Badhams are suggesting: that Mark claims that "his sources" had kept to themselves their knowledge of the empty tomb until they finally broke their silence and told him. It is much more believable and in line with ordinary narrative conventions to interpret as *temporary* silence the comment "they said nothing to anyone."

Second, as we shall see, Mark's closing comment is open to various explanations, which do not postulate that Mark had to insert that comment, because he had fashioned the whole empty tomb story and was consciously adding a "new element to the generally received traditions" about Jesus' destiny.

Third, the redaction-critical studies of Mark's Gospel published in recent decades have convincingly established that the evangelist was no wooden mouthpiece of the traditions he received.[5] He showed a certain measure of liberty and inventiveness in arranging and embellishing those traditions. But I do not think the weight of evidence from those redactional studies supports the view that Mark could simply invent *ex nihilo* an important item like the discovery of Jesus' empty tomb. In using and embellishing his sources, the evangelist was free but not that free.

Fourth, in advancing their hypothesis the Badhams pay no attention to redactional (and compositional) criticism. I do not know any scholar who has examined Mk 16:1–8 to distinguish the source(s) from the Markan redaction, and who then argues that for these eight verses Mark had *no source* but freely composed the narrative on his own. With some minor variations, a fairly general consensus is that the traditional source used (and added to) by the evangelist ran as follows:

> On the first day of the week Mary Magdalene, and Mary the mother of James, and Salome went to the tomb when the sun had risen. They saw that the stone had been rolled back and entering they saw a young man sitting on the right side, dressed

in a white robe and they were amazed. And he said to them, "Do not be amazed. You seek Jesus of Nazareth who was crucified. He has risen. He is not here. See the place where they laid him." And they went out and fled, for trembling and astonishment had come upon them.[6]

Redactional criticism supports the existence of a pre-Markan source and not the Badhams' thesis that Mark composed *ex nihilo* the entire empty tomb story. It is a little too obvious that by denying any traditional (and historical) source for Mk 16:1–8, the Badhams can more easily commend their view that immortality of the soul rather than bodily resurrection is the real Christian hope.

Before turning to more theological interpretations of Mk 16:8c, we should note other somewhat "historical" versions of the evangelist's purpose here. By emphasizing the women's frightened silence, Mark intends to indicate that the appearances of the risen Jesus and not the discovery of the empty tomb had first triggered faith in the resurrection. The silence of the women "explains" why such an important sign of Jesus' resurrection as his empty grave did not play a role as the original basis for Easter faith and in the first preaching (see, for example, 1 Cor 15:3b–5 where two appearances but not the discovery of the empty tomb figure in the resurrection kerygma cited by Paul). In other words, Mark introduces the theme of the women's silence, so as to respect and account for what he took to be historical facts: Peter, the twelve and other male disciples had played the foundational role in preaching the resurrection of the crucified Jesus, the women's role was relatively unimportant, and the story of their discovering the empty tomb entered the Easter message only later.[7]

There might be some truth in these historicizing comments on Mk 16:8c. Yet, as Eduard Schweizer comments, to see Mk 16:8 as "an attempt to explain how it happened that so much time passed before there was any report of the discovery of the empty tomb is too modern a suggestion. A critically trained historian would think this way but not the early Christian Church."[8] Furthermore, merely historical hypotheses about the women's reactions lack connection with theological themes that surface earlier in Mark's text. They aim at explaining the cryptic reference to the women's silence in terms of what we know "extrinsically" from Paul, Acts and other New Testament books, instead of first looking for some clue in what Mark himself has already written. What "theological truth" is Mark "attempting to express when he reports the silence of the women"?[9]

2. *Theological Explanations.* One well-argued thesis about the women's fearful silence comes in Willi Marxsen's redactional study, *Mark the Evangelist* (Nashville, 1969).[10] His thesis takes as its background the much discussed Markan phenomenon of the "messianic secret."

(a) Right from the first chapter of Mark's Gospel we come across the tension or even "contradiction" between an injunction to silence and its transgression (Mk 1:40–45). Marxsen attributes these "contradictions" to the redactional work of the evangelist who aims at expressing the tension between concealment and disclosure or between silence and speech. The "contradiction" between the command to spread the news of the resurrection in Mk 16:7 and the women's fearful silence in Mk 16:8 results from the evangelist's redactional work, specifically in that he inserts 16:7 into his source. In the case of Mk 16:7–8 the order to spread the news comes first, the silence second, whereas during Mark's account of Jesus' ministry the order is normally the reverse: Jesus asks for silence but others give way to a compulsion to speak (*Mark the Evangelist,* p. 91).

Marxsen's work in redaction criticism gave new life to the thesis of the messianic secret initiated by William Wrede's 1901 work, *Das Messiasgeheimnis in den Evangelien.* Wrede had argued that the earthly Jesus never claimed to be Messiah, and that Mark read back into that story of the ministry later messianic beliefs. Marxsen's redactional techniques distinguished more successfully between the evangelist's work and his traditional sources. At the same time,

Marxsen recognized the real theological nature of Mark's Gospel. All of this meant that Marxsen could fit the question of Mk 16:8c into a framework of explanation for the whole Gospel.

Nevertheless, one wonders whether as such the "messianic secret" can bear the weight assigned to it. There is much to be said for finding Mark's theological thrust in the theme of the *revelation:* the revelation of the kingdom (Mk 1:1–8:21) and then the revelation of the destiny of the Son of Man (Mk 8:22ff). Or else one could stress more the revelations of Jesus as the Son of God, a revelation which reaches its climax in the centurion's confession (Mk 15:39).

Where Marxsen's interpretation of Mk 16:7–8 becomes really doubtful is when he develops the work of some earlier scholars and links the two verses to the *parousia* that Mark expects to occur soon in Galilee, the land of preaching and the messianic secret.

Mark writes in the sixties; he wishes to direct the Christian community to gather in Galilee for the glorious coming of the Lord. Unlike the *ōphthē* ("he appeared") of 1 Cor 15:5–8 which is a technical term for *resurrection* appearances, the *opsesthe* ("you will see") of Mk 16:7 points to the *parousia* that the evangelist (wrongly) supposes is about to occur in the sixties. Where the Messiah is proclaimed, an epiphany takes place and the *parousia* is anticipated (Mk 16:7; see also 14:28). But, in Mark's scheme, for the moment the Messiah remains hidden, the epiphany is secret and the *parousia* is anticipated in quiet concealment (Mk 16:8). All this entails interpreting the women's silent fear (Mk 16:8c) in the context of the evangelist's message about an impending *parousia* in Galilee (*ibid.,* pp. 83–94).

A number of considerations tell against this view. Marxsen takes "Galilee" in the rest of Mark's Gospel to be a theological term symbolizing the place of preaching and/or the Gentile mission of the early Church. He must suppose that in Mk 14:28 and 16:7 it reverts to the status of a geographical term. Second, from the rest of his Gospel (despite 9:1; ch. 13; 14:62) it is not so clear that Mark expects an imminent *parousia*.[11] Third, other evidence is lacking to establish any special connection between Galilee and the *parousia*. Fourth, Mark presents the predictions of the Son of Man's passion and resurrection (8:31; 9:31; 10:32–34) separately from passages which can be interpreted as conveying—among other things— predictions of the *parousia* (ch. 13). Elsewhere in his Gospel Mark keeps the themes of resurrection and *parousia* apart. It is then hardly to be expected that he will mix them in ch. 16 by combining an announcement of an imminent *parousia* (to occur in the late sixties) with an account of women on Easter day (more than thirty years before) discovering the tomb of Jesus to be open and empty and hearing an angelic announcement of his resurrection. Fifth, we can interpret the words "he is going before you to Galilee" (Mk 16:7) in two ways: either (a) "he is going *at your head* (like a shepherd leading his sheep) to Galilee," or (b) "he is going *in advance of you* with a view to a rendezvous in Galilee." Explanation (a) seems more likely, inasmuch as it recalls the theme of Mk 14:27ff, the apostasy of the twelve and of Peter in particular. The shepherd's flock will be scattered, but this process will be reversed when the flock is reassembled. In either case the "going before" as such does not evoke any thoughts of the *parousia*. Sixth, R.H. Fuller adds a further point against Marxsen's position:

> The decisive argument which proves it to be, in Mark 16:7, a resurrection rather than a parousia reference is the naming of Peter as well as the disciples, a circumstance which indicates clearly that the Evangelist is alluding to the two appearances, listed in 1 Corinthians 15:5. If Mark 16:7 were pointing forward to the parousia, it is hard to see why Peter should be singled out for special mention. But if it points to resurrection appearances, the reason for the mention of Peter is obvious. [12]

Seventh, the verb "see" used in Mk 16:7 can refer to human beings experiencing the *parousia* (Mk 13:26; 1 Jn 3:2). But it can also be used of a vision of the risen Christ (1 Cor 9:1; Jn 20:18). Moreover, the seeing of Jesus in Mk 13:6–27 is to be preceded by war, famine, the emergence of false messiahs, the martyrdom of some disciples and other signs of which there is not a hint in Mk 16:7 and its immediate context. Finally, Marxsen himself has become more tentative about his view that Mk 16:7 points to an imminent *parousia* rather than an imminent post-resurrection appearance or appearances.[13]

Thus Marxsen has left us with the "messianic secret's" tension of disclosure/concealment as the way to understand the three women's fearful silence in Mk 16:8c. In *The Resurrection of Jesus of Nazareth,* where he treated the final section of Mark, Marxsen failed to raise the question of the duration of the women's silence (only temporary? or really permanent?) and lightly touched another theme that Norman Perrin was to develop. Marxsen presented the women as by their silence *"disobeying* the command given to them by the young men (whom we are undoubtedly intended to think of as an angel)" (p. 42; italics mine). A few years earlier, in *The Gospel Message of St. Mark* (Oxford, 1950), R.H. Lightfoot had reported questions about the fear, "silence and disobedience" of the women (pp. 85, 89). He replied by commenting that such questions as "whether the women conquered their fear or how long they remained silent were simply not in the mind of the evangelist" (p. 92). It may have been good, however, right from the outset to avoid the word "disobedience," a loaded term that as such already suggests a position on the silent flight of the women. This theme of disobedience emerges more fully in Perrin's *The Resurrection Narratives* (London, 1977). To that we can now turn.

(b) Perrin correctly connects the story of the women at Jesus' empty tomb (Mk 16:1–8) with two other narratives (Mk 15:40–41; 15:42–47). These three narratives (which deal with women, respectively, at the cross, at the burial of Jesus and at his tomb) are closely related—not least by the fact that two of the three women named in 15:40 turn up again in 15:47 and all three are again named in 16:1. Perrin notes the progressive failure of Jesus' male disciples that begins at Mk 6:52 and reaches its climax in the passion story with Judas' betrayal and Peter's denial of Jesus (pp. 30–31). Meanwhile women enter Mark's story (from 14:3–9) and "take over the role" one "might have expected to be played" by the male disciples (p. 31). They remain faithfully present at Jesus' death and burial and "are prepared to play their role in anointing him." It is "to their great honour to discover the empty tomb and the fact of the resurrection."

Then like the male disciples before them, "the women also fail their master" and "fail their trust" by not delivering "the message entrusted to them." Mark's Gospel ends[14] with total "discipleship failure," as "every disciple fails the master" (pp. 32–33). Perrin admits that this is a "grim picture" and a "dark" and "stark" vision of what Mark intends by the frightened silence of the owmen (p. 33). But is this picture of total failure on the part of all disciples, both male *and female,* the right vision to be drawn from Mk 16:8c?

Perrin rested his case without discussing "why Mark paints this grim picture" (p.33) and thinks of total "discipleship failure." The theme as a whole must await discussion or another occasion" (p. 35). Sadly Perrin died before being able to complete his case and suggest why Mark paints this grim picture. But does the evangelist in fact do so? As Perrin himself recognized, Mark writes his Gospel "to express the conviction that Jesus is the Christ, the Son of God," pursuing this theme from 1:1 "to the climactic confession of the centurion at the cross in 15:39" (pp. 34–35). After developing such a positive theme right through his work, it seems strange for Mark to conclude with a bleak, grim picture of total failure by all the disciples. Second, after the betrayal of Judas (14:10–11), the warning about the failure of the male disciples (14:27), their flight at the time of Jesus' arrest (14:50) and Peter's triple denial of his master (14:29–31; 66–72), the evangelist is hardly introducing a parallel to all that in the three women's silent flight from the empty tomb. Third, the women who had "followed" Jesus in Galilee (Mk 15:41) clearly personify a discipleship that remains faithful to the end. It would be very odd to cancel that picture suddenly in the last verse of the Gospel. Fourth, the most effective response to Perrin's theory of total failure remains, of course, a successful alternate explanation of the women's silent and fearful flight.[15] That we can find in an updated version of R.H. Lightfoot's comments.

Before we take up Lightfoot, however, we should note that Perrin's negative presentation of the women's silence in Mk 16:8c comes from a tendency of certain scholars to over-emphasize that Gospel's negative characterization of Jesus' disciples.[16] T.J. Weeden's *Mark: Traditions in Conflict* (Philadelphia, 1971) constitutes the high-point in the attempt to argue for a Markan attack on the twelve disciples. Weeden, in fact, holds that Mark is "assiduously involved in a vendetta against the disciples. He is intent on totally discrediting them" (p. 50). Such "a polemic against the disciples," as Rudolf Pesch points out, is pure speculation which has no basis.[17] Quentin Quesnell dismisses Weeden's thesis as "simply wrong"; "so much of the Marcan material simply does not fit the thesis."[18] Schuyler Brown shows that Weeden "is led to adopt highly improbable textual interpretation, with the result that his work as a whole fails to be convincing." In particular, his "interpretation of the empty-tomb narrative" is simply "bizarre."[19] To the extent that critics have effectively rejected the major voice for the theory of a Markan attempt to discredit the (male) disciples, the particular thesis of Perrin about the three women being part of an *overall* scheme of discipleship failure will not hold up. He cannot sustain that Mark wishes to paint a "grim picture" of the women, if Mark has no such "dark" and "stark" vision of the male disciples. Granted that the promise of Mk 16:7 ("tell his disciples and Peter that he is going before you to Galilee; there you will see him, as he told you") entails some kind of special rehabilitation of the *male* disciples, it would be strange for the evangelist in the very next verse suddenly to introduce a "grim picture" of the women whose record from 14:3 to 16:1ff—unlike that of the male disciples—has been consistently positive. Their fearful silence in 16:8c must have some meaning other than final failure. Let us see what Lightfoot makes of it.

(c) In *The Gospel Message of St. Mark*, Lightfoot explains the three women's fear in Mk 16:8c not as "fear of men, whether fear of the Jews or of the disciples' reaction to their message, if they gave it." To end the Gospel with "the thought of the fear of men" would be an intolerable anti-climax and utterly unworthy of St. Mark." "The whole tenor" of 16:5–8 suggests that what we are facing is rather "fear or dread of God . . . fear caused by revelation" which produces the women's amazement, flight, trembling, astonishment and silence (p. 88). In accounting for the women's emotions and reactions in Mk 16:5–8, Lightfoot points to a similar earlier episode in the Gospel, the stilling of the storm (4:35–41). There the disciples' "earlier physical alarm is now replaced by a much deeper fear." He notes the parallel between the silence of the women in 16:8c and the "bewildered utterance of the disciples" in 4:41 and adds: these reactions "arise from the same cause, namely, an increasing and involuntary realization of the nature and being of Him with whom they have to do" (*ibid.*). In the first case the men "were afraid with a great fear," but said something: "Who then is this, that even the wind and the sea obey him?" In the second case the women were simply "afraid," but said nothing. Yet Lightfoot is correct in seeing some parallel between the human reactions in both cases.

Even though the second passion prediction in Mk 9:32 ("they understood not the saying and were afraid to ask him") is almost a case in point, Lightfoot admits that, apart from 16:8c, we do not have a clear example where the evangelist explicitly refers "to silence as the result of fear of God, or, in other words, of revelation" (*ibid.*). He suggests a reason why Mark introduces "the combination of fear and silence" only in "the last sentence of the book." The evangelist treats with reserve both the crucifixion and its counterpart in the resurrection hinting at "the unspeakable tragedy and darkness of the Passion" and "the ineffable wonder and mystery" of the resurrection. One can appreciate, therefore, why Mark could lay a unique emphasis "upon the devastating results, for the women, of the first intimations of the greatest and final manifestation of the divine activity recorded" in his book (p. 89). Episodes of revelation earlier in Mark's Gospel produce "fear or astonishment or both together" in the disciples or others (pp. 90–91). In a climactic way "the reaction of the women at the tomb, their amazement, trembling, astonishment, fear" and silence "gathers up the emotions caused" earlier by the revelatory presence of God conveyed by Jesus' actions and teaching.[20]

In his own way and without reference to Lightfoot's *The Gospel Message of St. Mark*, Pesch finds in the women's silence of Mk 16:8c "a motif of reaction to the reception of revelation in accounts of epiphanies." To substantiate this claim he refers to such texts as 1 Sam 3:15 and Dan 7:28 (p. 536; see also p. 522) whereas Lightfoot exemplifies the connection between some revealing message from God and human silence by pointing to Ez 3:26; 24:27; Lk 1:20 and 2 Cor 12:4 (p. 87). Pesch rightly notes that the fear, trembling and flight of the three women are apocalyptic themes—he refers to Dan 7:15,28; 8:17,27 and 10:7—"which underline the meaning of the angel's *revelatory* message" (p. 528; italics mine). The "overwhelming secret" communicated by the angel in the announcement of Jesus' resurrection (Mk 16:6) produces trembling, ecstatic amazement and silence. Such a reaction emphasizes the *mysterium tremendum* of God's unexpected revelation. The women plan to anoint the corpse of the crucified Jesus. Instead they are "confronted with the message of his resurrection and are torn away from" their normal ways of thinking (Pesch, p. 535).

Pesch might have used the entire phrase from Rudolf Otto, *mysterium tremendum et fascinans*. The women go to the tomb (Mk 16:1–2), drawn unconsciously by the "fascinating mystery" of God about to be revealed to them. They flee from the tomb (Mk 16:8), shocked by the awe-inspiring message of Jesus' resurrection. The double-sided activity of the women exemplifies very well Otto's classic thesis about the human reaction to God and the revelation of the divine mystery. Second, Pesch comments curiously that Mark's reader, confronted with the account of the women's reaction to the "epiphany of God" that has taken place in Jesus' resurrection, is "invited to let himself be *fascinated* into faith" (p. 541; italics mine). Here Pesch recalls—for the case of the Gospel's *reader*—the *fascinans* from Otto's phrase, but ignores the *tremendum*. Surely the reader is invited to imitate the women by being fascinated *and* awe-inspired, and so come to faith (or be strengthened in an Easter faith that already exists)?

3. *Conclusion.* In interpreting Mk 16:8 our exegetical choices narrow down to these alternatives. Is the *fear* of the women a fear of human beings or of God? Is their *silence* to be interpreted as disobedience to the angel's command or as religious awe in the face of what has been revealed to them? Does their *flight* parallel the male disciples' flight of Mk 14:50 and represent the final stage in the despairing collapse of the disciples announced by Jesus in Mk 14:27,[21] or does it express a primordial terror at a divine intervention in our world (see Mk 5:14)? In short, does Mark want his readers to take a negative or a positive view of the women's fear, silence and flight?

Those who opt for the negative view can do so because they mistakenly apply to the three women the pattern of blindness and misunderstanding developed around the male disciples in Mk 8:27–10:52. The warning "you will all be scandalized" (Mk 14:27) is addressed to the men, not the women. In Mk 14:50 the male disciples desert Jesus and Peter goes on to deny him, but from Mk 14:2 to 16:1ff the record of the women has been consistently good. One may not simply transfer to the women the bleak picture Mark has painted of the male disciples (who, in any case, are promised a rehabilitation in Mk 14:28 and 16:7).

Lightfoot's positive interpretation of the women's silent and fearful flight in Mk 16:8 has backing from the pattern the evangelist has established throughout his Gospel. In a climactic way the reaction of the women gathers up feelings evoked by earlier episodes of divine *revelation* communicated by Jesus' *words* and *deeds*.

One might add that Mark establishes this theme right from the outset of the ministry. People are "astonished" at Jesus' teaching (Mk 1:22) and "amazed" at his power over unclean spirits (Mk 1:27).

Divine revelation reaches its climax in the event of the resurrection which produces the empty tomb (Mk 16:4–5)—a deed clarified and announced by the word (Mk 16:6). Faced with the uniquely great revelation of God in the resurrection of the crucified Jesus, the silent and fearful flight of the women is not only understandable but also highly appropriate.

A Personal Postscript

This book has singled out and examined several central questions that arise from the Easter testimony of St. Paul and the Gospel writers. What do the letters of Paul indicate about the form and nature of the post-resurrection appearances (Chapter 1)? What can we conclude from the Gospels and other sources about the role of Mary Magdalene as an Easter witness (Chapter 2)? How should we interpret Lk 24:42–43 which presents the risen Jesus as eating fish (Chapter 3)? What does Mark mean by the fear and silence of the women with which he ends his Gospel (Chapter 4)?

Once again I want to insist that a complete interpretation of Christ's resurrection would need to exercise the three styles of theologizing sketched in the introduction. In appropriating the Easter mystery one needs to consult not only the scholars but also the sufferers and the worshipers. It is, for example, eminently worthwhile drawing on biblical exegesis to reach some well-based historical conclusions about the post-resurrection appearances. At the same time, however, the risen Jesus also appears to us in the person of the poor and the dehumanized. He shows himself as well through common worship and private prayer. In short, scholarly research into the special, post-Easter appearances is indispensable. Yet we neglect at our peril the other ways in which the risen Lord "appears" and continues to reveal himself.

After *The Resurrection of Jesus Christ* (1973; published in England as *The Easter Jesus*), *What Are They Saying About the Resurrection?* (1978) and *Jesus Risen* (1987), this is my fourth work dedicated to questions surrounding Christ's victory over death. Other books of mine have contained chapters on the resurrection: *Man and His New Hopes* (1969), *Foundations of Theology* (1971), *The Theology of Secularity* (1974), *Faith under Fire* (1974), *Interpreting Jesus* (1983), *Finding Jesus* (1983) and *Jesus Today* (1986). It may be time to fall silent. Christ's resurrection remains far more than the sum of all our words.

Before imitating Mark's three women in their reaction to the Easter mystery, I would like to note how my language about the resurrection may have proved more successful than some of my arguments. Since 1972 I have put the case for identifying his Easter testimony as the major (but not the only) clue for interpreting St. Peter and the Petrine mystery. To my disappointment this thesis has not been debated. The only major response so far has come from Francis Fiorenza who in his *Foundational Theology* (New York, 1984) misreported my thesis as being a claim about the foundation of the Church. (See my comments in *Heythrop Journal* 26 [1985] pp. 177–78 and 201.) A phrase I adopted in justifying Easter faith, "the experiential correlate" (*The Resurrection of Jesus Christ,* pp. 69–73), has been taken up in later works like William Thompson's *The Jesus Debate* (New York, 1985, pp. 227–28) and Peter Carnley's *The Structure of Resurrection Belief* (Oxford, 1987, p. 264). In *The Nature of Christian Belief* (London, 1986, p. 18) the House of Bishops of the General Synod of the Church of England made use of the title of my book *The Easter Jesus*.

But this is enough by way of a self-indulgent retrospect. There is a time to fall silent like those friends of Gandalf in *The Lord of the Rings* when the old man quite unexpectedly returned: "Between wonder, joy and fear they stood and found no words to say." An awed silence may be the best homage one can pay to the great mystery of Easter, which is both Jesus' victory over death and the beginning of the end of the world.

Notes

Chapter 1

1. *New Testament Theology,* vol. 1, *The Proclamation of Jesus* (London, 1971), p. 308.
2. *Journal of Biblical Literature* 100 (1981), pp. 415–32.
3. Vol. 32A (New York, 1984), pp. 250–51.
4. *1 and 2 Corinthians.* New Century Bible (London, 1971), p. 196.
5. See, for example, R.E. Brown, *The Gospel According to John XIII–XXI.* Anchor Bible, vol. 29A (New York, 1970), pp. 999, 1003, 1008, 1017; J. Jeremias, *The Proclamation of Jesus,* pp. 307–08.
6. On this see further my *Interpreting Jesus* (London and Ramsey, 1983), pp. 116–20.
7. Kessler quotes with approval the words of Peter Stuhlmacher about the appearances being a "becoming visible of Jesus who has been crucified and called by God into the life of the end times" (p. 149). In 1 Cor 15:5,6–7 the use of the formula *ōphthē* with the dative denotes the end of history, the "final, definitive saving presence of God that is manifested" in the appearances (p. 153; see p. 151).

Chapter 2

1. "Witness" is often used in contemporary English in much the same way it is used in the Bible; cf. *The New International*

Dictionary of New Testament Theology, ed. Colin Brown (Grand Rapids, 1978). The two definitions which interest us concern the actual testimony and the one who gives the testimony.

2. Flavius Josephus, *Antiquities* (4,8,15), tr. H. St. J. Thackeray (New York, 1930), pp. 580–81. That women are not qualified as witnesses is an old and generally held (therefore anonymously transmitted) principle; see especially Mishnah *Shebueoth* 4:1; cf. Dt 19:17 (H.L. Strack and P. Billerbeck, *Kommentar zum NT aus Talmud und Midrasch* 3 [Munich, 1926] 560c). Only in those very seldom and very urgent cases, where *one* witness only is sufficient, is a woman admitted as a witness (see Mishnah, Rosh ha-Shanah 1:8; also *Encyclopedia Judaica* 16, 586).

3. Milan Machoveč, *A Marxist Looks at Jesus* (Philadelphia, 1976), pp. 168–69.

4. Origen, Contra Celsum, 2, 55 (tr. H. Chadwick [Cambridge, 1953], pp. 109–10).

5. Ernest Renan, *Vie de Jésus* (Paris, 1863), pp. 434–35. He believed that the strong personality of Jesus and the passionate love Mary had for him led her to assert that he had risen.

6. Leo the Great, *De ascensione Domini serm.* 2,4 (SC 74, 141–42).

7. Gregory the Great, *De apparitione Christi Magdalenae facta* (Patrum opuscula selecta 2, hom. 25 [Innsbruck, 1892], 189).

8. Hippolytus of Rome, *De Cantico* 24–26 (CSCO 264, 43–49).

9. Giuseppe Ricciotti, *The Life of Christ* (Milwaukee, 1947). Ricciotti concedes the fact that the women around Jesus were faithful and generous, and that Mary Magdalene is the first named by the three Synoptic writers as visiting the grave of Jesus after his burial (pp. 650–51). Although she and the other women found the tomb empty and encountered the angel(s) who announced that Jesus had risen and asked them to spread the news, nevertheless, later, even after the apostles and the entire Church were convinced that Jesus had risen, there was a prejudice against appealing to the testimony of women

(p. 653). Ricciotti believes that the early Church acted thus for prudent reasons: not to give Jews and idolators the impression that too much credence was placed in over-imaginative women given to spreading tales (*ibid.*). More recently than Ricciotti, Francesco Spadafora (*La risurrezione di Gesù* [Rovigo, 1978], p. 204) argues that the appearance to Mary Magdalene is not as important as those to the apostles—the Jerusalem appearances are not as important as those in Galilee—since those in Galilee are connected with the foundation of the Church.

10. Joseph Fitzmyer, *The Gospel according to Luke* (X–XXIV) (Garden City, N.Y., 1985), pp. 1535–37.

11. Raymond Brown, *The Gospel according to St. John* (XIII–XXI), p. 988.

12. Rudolf Bultmann, *The Gospel of John* (Philadelphia, 1971), p. 686.

13. Edwyn Hoskyns, *The Fourth Gospel* (London, 1947), p. 542.

14. C.H. Dodd, *The Interpretation of the Fourth Gospel* (Cambridge, 1953), p. 440.

15. C.K. Barrett, *The Gospel according to St. John* (London, 1955), p. 466.

16. J.H. Bernard, *The Gospel according to John* (Edinburgh, 1928), p. 671. A different emphasis is given to 1 Cor 15 by Hans Conzelmann (*1 Corinthians* [Philadelphia, 1975]), who believes that Paul mentioned only those appearances which fit his purpose in writing this epistle. "The first appearance, to Cephas . . . is not recorded in the Gospels and only alluded to in one passage, Lk 24:34. Historically speaking, it was the reason for the status of Peter in the primitive church and probably for the founding of the circle of the Twelve. The latter is then legitimized by a further appearance. That the circle arose only after the death of Jesus is already plain from the number: that Jesus appeared to 'the Twelve' " (pp. 256–57). This last assertion certainly does not enjoy universal acceptance. An example

of someone who holds the opposite view is Ben F. Meyer (*The Aims of Jesus* [London, 1979], pp. 153–54): "The historicity of the deliberate act of choosing twelve disciples to participate most intimately in his mission (Mark 3:13f. par.; 6:7–13 par.; cf. Matt. 19:28 par.) is beyond reasonable doubt. . . ." "Jesus, moreover, made the twelve more than a sign of the future. He gave them a share in its coming-to-be, by sending them (Mark 6:7 parr.) in groups of two (Mark 6:7) to enlist Israel's welcome of the reign of God (Mark 3:14; Matt. 10:7; Luke 9:2)."

17. See my previous chapter. The main reason Kessler concentrates on Paul is that he has doubts about the reliability of the Gospel accounts (cf. pp. 117–18, 121).

18. William Thompson, *The Jesus Debate* (New York, 1985), p. 222.

19. Two prominent contemporary theologians who would agree that the appearances are extremely important are Walter Kasper (*Jesus the Christ* [New York, 1976]) and Hans Küng (*On Being a Christian* [Garden City, N.Y., 1976]). Kasper says (p. 129): "I have already mentioned the irreconcilable divergences between the kerygmatic tradition and the Easter stories. But the two traditions are not unified within themselves. . . . In spite of these irreconcilable divergences all traditions agree on one thing: Jesus appeared to certain disciples after his death; he proved himself living and was proclaimed to have risen from the dead. This is the centre, the core, where all traditions meet." Küng asserts (pp. 348–49): "But a reduction of all the appearances—to the twelve (the controlling body in Jerusalem), to James (the brother of Jesus), to all the disciples (the greater circle of missionaries), to more than five hundred brethren, to Paul himself—to the one appearance to Peter, as if the former were merely to confirm the latter, is not justified by these or other texts." Küng grants that there might be and probably are elaborations in the Gospel appearance stories, but he adds (p. 364): "Perhaps the series of witnesses in its original form could even be reduced to that one

woman whom all the Gospels unanimously present as a single witness and whom John makes the sole witness: Mary Magdalene (Mary, the mother of Jesus, oddly enough, plays no part at all among the witnesses of the resurrection)."

20. A typical example of one who diminishes the importance of the appearance to women over against those to the male disciples is M.-J. Lagrange (*Evangile selon saint Marc* [Paris, 1929]). He proposes three categories of appearances: the first to the apostles and disciples, the second to the women who had supported him, and the third to his mother. In this scheme the appearance(s) to Mary Magdalene (Jn 20:1–8) and her companion (Mt 28:9–10) become rewards for fidelity and mere preparations for the appearances that are truly significant for the Church and her teaching: these are to the male apostles and disciples (p. 449).

21. Rudolf Schnackenburg, *The Gospel according to St. John,* vol. 3 (New York, 1982).

22. Z.C. Hodges, "The Women and the Empty Tomb," *Bibliotheca sacra* 13 (1966), p. 309.

23. Hubert Ritt, "Die Frauen und die Osterbotschaft," *Die Frau im Urchristentum* (Freiburg, 1983), pp. 117–33.

24. *Ibid.,* p. 130.

25. *Ibid.*

26. *Ibid.,* p. 131.

27. *Ibid.,* pp. 131–32.

28. *Ibid.,* p. 132.

29. *Ibid.,* p. 133.

30. François Bovon, "Le privilège pascal de Marie-Madeleine," *New Testament Studies* 30 (1984), pp. 50–62.

31. *Ibid.,* p. 51.

32. *Ibid.,* pp. 51–52.

33. *Ibid.,* p. 52.

34. Elisabeth Schüssler-Fiorenza, *In Memory of Her* (New York, 1983).

35. Schüssler-Fiorenza does not distinguish between the appear-

ances (1) which took place in Galilee and (2) those in Jerusalem. Instead she simply says: "Whereas Matthew, John, and
the Markan appendix credit primacy of apostolic witness to
Mary Magdalene, the Jewish Christian pre-Pauline confession
in 1 Cor 15:3–6 and Luke claim that the resurrected Lord
appeared first to Peter. Since the tradition of Mary Magdalene's primacy in apostolic witness challenged the Petrine tradition, it is remarkable that it has survived in two independent
streams of the Gospel tradition. Moreover, later apocryphal
writings—as we have seen—reflect the theological debate over
the apostolic primacy of Mary Magdalene and Peter explicitly"
(p. 332). We should note, however, that biblical commentators more commonly classify the appearances as those (to Peter
and others) in Galilee and those (to Mary Magdalene and
others) in Jerusalem (cf. Raymond Brown, "John 21 and the
First Appearance of the Risen Jesus to Peter," *Resurrexit*
[Rome, 1974], p. 246).

36. Bovon says (p. 50) that in the early Church the traditions about
Mary Magdalene outside of Scripture were filled in and distorted
not by the supporters of the universal Church but by various
marginal movements such as Gnosticism and Encratism. Raymond Brown and others note that the tradition of an appearance
to him probably provided the original context or catalyst for
much New Testament material about Peter. The theme of Peter
as receiver of special revelations was greatly developed in the
apocrypha (cf. Raymond Brown et al., *Peter in the New Testament*
[New York, 1973]), p. 165). The Marcan appendix (16:9–20)
states that the risen Jesus appeared *first* to Mary Magdalene (Mk
16:9)—the only place in the New Testament where a chrono-
logical order of appearance is clearly mentioned. The dating of
this appendix varies. Tischendorf, citing Irenaeus and
Hippolytus, believes that it was already known in the second
century (Constantinus Tischendorf, *Novum Testamentum graece* 1
[Leipzig, 1869], pp. 406–7), while Metzger notes that "the

traditional ending of Mark, so familiar through the AV and
other translations of the Textus Receptus, is present in the vast
number of witnesses. . . . The earliest patristic witnesses to
part or all of the long ending are Irenaeus and the Diatessaron.
It is not certain whether Justin Martyr was acquainted with the
passage; in his *Apology* (1:45) he includes five words that occur,
in a different sequence, in ver. 20" (Bruce Metzger, *A Textual
Commentary on the Greek New Testament* [London and New York,
1971], p. 124). The Marcan appendix, thus composed at the
same time the Gnostic writers were disseminating their views,
gives priority to the appearance to Mary Magdalene. C.S. Mann
is more or less in agreement with the opinion of Tischendorf and
Metzger. In his commentary on Mk 16:9–20 in the Anchor
Bible series (*Mark* [Garden City, N.Y., 1986]) he writes: "In
fact, in all the literature before the middle of the fourth century
there are only two possible allusions to this anonymous ending.
The first is in Justin Martyr (*Apology* 1:45): 'Going out, his
apostles proclaimed' (or 'made a proclamation') 'everywhere.'
The second is from Irenaeus, cited in Latin: 'At the end of his
Gospel, Mark says, "And so the Lord Jesus, after he had spoken
to them, was received into heaven, and sits at the right hand of
the Father" ' "(p. 674). Concerning vss. 9–11 of the Marcan
appendix, Vincent Taylor's (*The Gospel according to St. Mark*
[New York, 1966], p. 610) brief comment is: "The vocabulary
and style of this section show clearly that it was not written by
Mark, but is based on a knowledge of traditions found in Lk and
Jn." Joseph Hug (*Le finale de l'Evangile de Marc* [Paris, 1978])
dates this ending of Mark's Gospel to the second third of the
second century (p. 214). He bases this judgment on the explicit
witness of Irenaeus and the *Diatessaron* (A.D. 180) and the
possible allusion by Justin Martyr and the *Epistola apostolorum*
(middle of second century). Elsewhere he concludes that (1) Mk
16:9–11 does not depend on Jn 20:14–18 nor Mt 18:9–10; (2)
Mk 16:9–11 comes from a common tradition underlying the

parallel accounts and known besides from the Jewish anti-Christian polemics; and (3) Mk 16:9–11 does not reflect the language nor does it reproduce the themes of any parallel Gospel accounts, yet its themes are secondary except for the stress on the unbelief and perhaps the position given to Mary (p. 165).

37. Pheme Perkins, *The Gnostic Dialogue* (New York, 1980), p. 205.

38. Pheme Perkins, *Resurrection: New Testament Witness and Contemporary Reflection,* p. 167.

38. Robert Grant, in his review of Schüssler-Fiorenza's book, goes so far as to call it "a wholehearted attempt to rewrite traditional Christian history in favor of a feminist version" (cf. Robert Grant, "The Reconstruction of Christian Origins," *Journal of Religion* 65 [1965], p. 83).

40. Perhaps Perkins more accurately should have said that Peter's primacy was "*largely* but not exclusively" based on his rallying the others after his vision of the risen Lord. Also, she ignores here Lk 24:34, not to mention Lk 22:32. Cf. Gerald O'Collins, "Peter as Easter Witness," *Heythrop Journal* 22 (1981), pp. 1–18.

Chapter 3

1. Some versions (for example, the RSV) translate *sunalizomenos* as "staying with" or as "being in the company of" the disciples (NEB). But the majority of commentators and translators favor "eating with" or "being at table with": for example, E. Haenchen, *The Acts of the Apostles: A Commentary* (Oxford, 1971), p. 141.

2. In his ICC volume *The Gospel According to St. Luke* (Edinburgh, 1896, 5th ed., 1922). A. Plummer comments on Lk 24:43 by asking: "Nothing is said here or in the meal at Emmaus about drinking, but are we to infer that nothing was drunk?" (p. 561). Plummer, who writes before form- and redaction-criticism

changed Gospel exegesis, may be nursing the presupposition, "You cannot have a proper meal unless there is also something to drink."

3. Anchor Bible, vol. 28A (New York, 1985).

4. The New International Greek Testament Commentary (Exeter, 1978).

5. The Tyndale New Testament Commentaries (Leicester, 1974). In *Das Evangelium Nach Lukas* RNT (Regensburg, 1955) J. Schmid likewise comments that while not needing any food, the risen Jesus dispelled the disciples' "unbelief" by truly eating the fish. "How he could take in this nourishment," Schmid admits, "remains for us a mystery" (p. 360). P. Benoit also agrees that Jesus ate the fish—not because his glorified body needed to eat, but because with "pedagogical condescension" he wanted to prove to his disciples that he could eat and was not a mere phantom (*Passion et Resurrection de Seigneur* [Paris, 1966], p. 323).

6. New International Commentary (Grand Rapids, 1981).

7. So also W. Grundmann, *Das Evangelium nach Lukas,* THKNT (Berlin, 1971), p. 448.

8. *Das Evangelium nach Lukas,* RNT (Regensburg, 1977), p. 668.

9. In "Paul's Conversion/Call: A Comparative Analysis of the Three Reports in Acts," C.W. Hedrick shows very well how in Luke's literary technique the three narratives from chapters 9, 22 and 26 "are composed so as to supplement, complement and *correct* one another" (*Journal of Biblical Literature* 100 [1981], pp. 415–32, at p. 432; italics mine). What Hedrick might have added is that Luke's corrective self-commentary can also work by "forewarning" the reader about the need to interpret carefully more spectacular scenarios to come later.

10. The Emmaus story should also have prepared the reader to be cautious about taking the fish-eating motif *au pied de la lettre.* The risen Jesus does not operate under the normal bodily conditions of this-worldly human beings: he appears and disappears at will; friends recognize him only when "their eyes" are

"opened" (Lk 24:15–16,31). Marshall argues that Luke realizes that the Emmaus story could lead readers astray and hence introduces items like the eating of fish to stress the "physical" side of resurrection: "If the previous story [24:13–35] has given the impression that the spiritual presence of Jesus is what ultimately matters, Luke redresses the balance in this narrative [24:36–43] in which the physical reality of the risen Jesus is heavily emphasized" (p. 900). But does Luke want to reduce the glorious (24:26), transformed bodiliness of Jesus to the state of a resuscitated corpse which eats and digests food?

11. Apropos of Lk 24:42–43, Grundmann interprets the evangelist's "apologetical meaning" to be simply this: "The bodily resurrection is so real that the Risen One can eat" (p. 451). But that is to miss the various ways Luke himself qualifies and corrects this way of portraying Jesus after his resurrection.

12. J.-M. Guillaume, *Luc interprète des anciennes traditions sur la résurrection de Jésus* (Paris, 1979), p. 136.

13. In *Die Apostelgeschichte des Lukas,* THHKNT vol. 5 (Berlin, 1983) G. Schille sees in Acts 10:41 "die Legitimation der Apostel" (p. 249).

14. See R. Fabris, *Atti degli Apostoli* (Rome, 1977), p. 69; J. Crowe, *The Acts,* New Testament Message, vol. 8 (Delaware, 1979), p. xxv.

15. X. Léon-Dufour, *Resurrection and the Message of Easter* (London, 1974), p. 167.

16. C.M. Martini, "Apparizioni agli apostoli in Lc 24, 36–43, nel complesso dell'opera lucana," *Resurrexit,* ed. E. Dhanis (Rome, 1974), pp. 241–42. Acts 10:41 recalls Lk 22:30 ("you will eat and drink at table in my kingdom"), language which suggests not only the joy of eternal life with God but also the banquet of the Eucharist.

17. Fabris, p. 341.

18. New Testament Message, vol. 5 (Delaware, 1980), p. 290. In part La Verdiere's interpretation echoes Richard Dillon's view

that in Lk 24:36–43 Jesus represents the missionary to whom
Christians should show hospitality: "the risen Christ seems to
reenact precisely the procedure he had prescribed for his itiner-
ant representatives." Dillon refers to the mission scheme of Lk
10:2–12 and finds a "remarkable analogy" between that missionary instruction and the appearance story (*From Eye-Witnesses to
Ministers of the Word* [Rome, 1978], p. 187). Lk 10:2–12 and
24:36–43 have some common features, above all the greeting of
peace and the eating. But unlike the missionaries of Lk 10:7,9,
the risen Christ does not come to stay; he does not drink nor
does he heal the sick. These and further differences cast doubt
on Dillon's claim that the "risen Christ appears in the role of
missionary to the chosen household" (*ibid.*, p. 188).

Chapter 4

1. Scholars agree that Mark's Gospel has been preserved only so far
   as 16:8. They disagree as to whether the evangelist meant to
   finish his Gospel at that point. In *The Gospel According to St Mark*
   (London, 1955) Vincent Taylor lists (a) those who maintain and
   (b) those who deny that Mark intended 16:8 as the conclusion of
   his Gospel (pp. 609–10). As we shall see, to (a) one should add
   Normann Perrin and to list (b) Eduard Schweizer. See further
   C.S. Mann, *Mark. A New Translation with Introduction and Commentary,* Anchor Bible 27 (New York, 1986), pp. 659–63. Like
   Perrin, Mann holds that Mark finished his Gospel at 16:8. John
   E. Alsup also sees Mark 16:1–8 as "the intended conclusion of
   this Gospel" (*The Post-Resurrection Appearance Stories of the Gospel
   Tradition* [Stuttgart, 1975], p. 88).
2. With the great majority of scholars, I presume here that Matthew and Luke used Mark as one of their major sources.
3. Almost twenty years before the Badhams, N.Q. Hamilton had
   also proposed that Mark himself had created the empty tomb
   story of 16:1–8 ("Resurrection Tradition and the Composition

of Mark," *Journal of Biblical Literature* 84 [1965], pp. 415–21; see Alsup, *Post-Resurrection Appearance,* p. 90, fn. 26).

4. Or do the Badhams want to attribute to Mark the claim to be an *omniscient* narrator? The woman never spoke to anyone, but the narrator knows the whole story.

5. On redaction criticism of Mark, see Mann, *Mark,* pp. 35–39.

6. In *Das Markusevangelium:* II Teil (Freiburg, 1977) Rudolf Pesch denies that Mk 16:7 is redactional (pp. 538–39) but he is one of the few to do so. In *The History of the Synoptic Tradition* (Oxford, 1963) Rudolf Bultmann called Mk 16:7 "a footnote put by Mark into the passage from the tradition, to prepare the way for a Galilean appearance of Jesus" (p. 285). Vincent Taylor followed this same view (*Gospel,* p. 608). Alsup also argues that Mark added 16:7 to the tradition he took over (*Post-Resurrection Appearance,* p. 92).

7. With varying nuances this is the view of G. Bornkamm, *Jesus of Nazareth* (London, 1960) p. 183; B.H. Branscomb, *Commentary on St Mark's Gospel,* Moffatt Commentaries (London, 1937), p. 309); R. Bultmann, *History of the Synoptic Tradition,* p. 285; H. Grass, *Ostergeschehen und Osterberichte* (2nd ed. Göttingen, 1962), pp. 22–23; V. Taylor, *The Life and Ministry of Jesus* (London, 1955), p. 223; J. Wellhausen, *Das Evangelium Marci* (Berlin, 1902), p. 136.

8. *The Good News According to Mark* (London, 1971), p. 368.

9. *Ibid.*

10. First published as *Der Evangelist Markus* (Göttingen, 1956).

11. One should note that in Mk 13:5–7 the *parousia* seems still rather a long way off.

12. *The Formation of the Resurrection Narratives* (London, 1972), pp. 63–64.

13. See his *The Resurrection of Jesus of Nazareth* (London, 1970), pp. 163–64; *Introduction to the New Testament* (London, 1968), pp. 141–42. Against Marxsen's thesis of an imminent *parousia* in Galilee, see also Pesch, *Markusevangelium* II, p. 540.

14. On pp. 20–22 Perrin argues convincingly that 16:8 was the intended ending for Mark's Gospel.

15. Unlike Perrin, Schweizer denies that Mk 16:8 is the intended ending of the Gospel and holds that "it is necessary to assume that the conclusion of the Gospel has been lost" (p. 366; see p. 373). Like Perrin, however, he interprets negatively the silent and fearful flight of the women in 16:8; even "those who are filled with devotion, who love Jesus and show a measure of courage" reveal a "complete lack of understanding." "Even the words of the angel produce nothing" in the women "but fear and terror; they do not evoke any faith or understanding." Nevertheless, Schweizer postulates that in an alleged lost conclusion to Mark, Jesus fulfilled the promise to go before his disciples and "accomplish what human hearts cannot do; despite every failure he would call the disciples again to discipleship and would encounter them in a way that would enable them to see him" (p. 373). Certainly by postulating a lost encounter between the risen Jesus and his disciples, Schweizer does not leave us with a totally grim picture of the disciples. All the same, is it correct to use Mk 8:27–10:52, which concerns the ignorance and blindness of the *male* disciples, to interpet the women's reaction in Mk 16:8? Neither earlier nor in that verse is there anything about the *women's* "total blindness" and "lack of understanding"—whether "complete" or otherwise. Once again, however, the best response (in this case to Schweizer's thesis") is to come up with a more convincing explanation of the women's silent and fearful flight.

16. See for example, J.B. Tyson, "The Blindness of the Disciples, "*Journal of Biblical Literature* 80 (1961), pp. 261–68; N. Perrin, "The Christology of Mark: A Study in Methodology," *Journal of Religion* 51 (1971), pp. 173–87. Among those who understand Mark to have written his Gospel as a polemic against some early Christians, Mann (*Mark,* p. 661) lists and criticizes not only T.J. Weeden but also J.D. Crossan and W. Kelber for whom the women's silence represents the Jerusalem community's fail-

ure to communicate the message of the resurrection. In this view the faith of Mk 16:1–7 confronts the failure of the Jerusalem community symbolized by Mk 16:8.

17. *Das Markusevangelium* II, p. 536, fn. 33.

18. Review in *Catholic Biblical Quarterly* 35 (1973), pp. 124, 125.

19. Review in *Theological Studies* 33 (1972), p. 755.

20. In Mark's Gospel the theme of "amazement" (which ranges from "astonishment" through "trembling" to "fear") occurs thirty-four times. The last few verses of Mark speak six times of various forms of "amazement" (Mk 16:5–8). See Pesch's excursus on the theme, *Markusevangelium* II, pp. 150–52. After being sympathetic toward Lightfoot's analysis of the women's fear, awe, terror and trembling, Mann finds "very negative connotations" in Mark's use of "they fled" (Mk 16:8c). But does flight always have very negative connotations in Mark? See, for example, Mk 13:14. Unlike Lightfoot, Mann does not interpret the women's fear as religious awe but as terror of human beings (the Romans? the Jewish authorities? the male disciples?). He argues that Mark wrote "for a community overtaken by fear [of human beings], a community which needed the reassurance that even those who were the first to hear of the vindication of Jesus in the Resurrection had been terrified [of human beings]" (p. 670).

21. In an article that is otherwise sympathetic to the women's role as Easter witnesses, Martin Hengel interprets the women's silent flight in Mk 16:8 as the "high-point" in the disciples' despair and collapse predicted by Mk 14:27 ("Maria Magdalena und die Frauen als Zeugen," in *Abraham unser Vater, Festschrift* for Otto Michel's sixtieth birthday, ed. O. Betz *et al.* [Leyden, 1963], p. 253).

Bibliography

Alsup, J.E., *The Post-Resurrection Appearance Stories of the Gospel-Tradition* (Stuttgart, 1975).

Brown, R.E., *The Gospel According to John XIII–XXI,* Anchor Bible, vol. 29A. (New York, 1970).

Carnley, P.F., *The Structure of Resurrection Belief* (Oxford, 1987).

Fitzmyer, J.A., *The Gospel According to Luke X–XXIV,* Anchor Bible, vol. 28A (New York, 1985).

Fuller, R.H., *The Formation of the Resurrection Narratives* (2d ed., Philadelphia, 1980).

Furnish, V.P., *II Corinthians,* Anchor Bible, vol. 32A (New York, 1984).

Kessler, H., *Sucht den Lebenden nicht bei den Toten* (Düsseldorf, 1985).

Lightfoot, R.H., *The Gospel Message of Mark* (Oxford, 1950).

Mann, C.S., *Mark,* Anchor Bible, vol. 27 (New York, 1986).

Marshall, I.H., *The Gospel of Luke* (Exeter, 1978).

Marxsen, W., *Mark the Evangelist* (Nashville, 1969).

———, *The Resurrection of Jesus of Nazareth* (London, 1970).

Perkins, P., *The Gnostic Dialogue* (New York, 1980).

———, *The Resurrection* (New York, 1984).

Perrin, N., *The Resurrection According to Matthew, Mark and Luke* (Philadelphia, 1977).

Pesch, R., *Das Markusevangelium,* vol. 2 (Freiburg, 1977).

Rahner, K., *Foundations of Christian Faith* (New York, 1978).

Schnackenburg, R., *The Gospel According to St. John,* vol. 3 (New York, 1982).
Schüssler, Fiorenza E., *In Memory of Her* (New York, 1983).
Thompson, W., *The Jesus Debate* (New York, 1985).

Note: these are among the most significant works referred to or discussed in this book.

Index of Names